First World War
and Army of Occupation
War Diary
France, Belgium and Germany

41 DIVISION
Headquarters, Branches and Services
Adjutant and Quarter-Master General
1 May 1916 - 30 August 1918

WO95/2620/2

The Naval & Military Press Ltd
www.nmarchive.com
Published in association with The National Archives

Published by

The Naval & Military Press Ltd

Unit 10 Ridgewood Industrial Park,

Uckfield, East Sussex,

TN22 5QE England

Tel: +44 (0) 1825 749494

www.naval-military-press.com

www.nmarchive.com

This diary has been reprinted in facsimile from the original. Any imperfections are inevitably reproduced and the quality may fall short of modern type and cartographic standards.

© Crown Copyright
Images reproduced by permission of The National Archives, London, England, 2015.

Contents

Document type	Place/Title	Date From	Date To
Heading	WO95/2620-2 41 Div A & Q Mar '18-July '18		
Heading	41 Div A & Q Branch Mar 1918-July From Italy		
War Diary	Italy	02/03/1918	02/03/1918
War Diary	France	10/03/1918	28/03/1918
Miscellaneous	41st Division. Court Martial Statement For Month Of March, 1918		
Miscellaneous	Full List Of Actual Casualties For Period 21st March to 1st April, 1918 Appendix 6	21/03/1918	21/03/1918
Operation(al) Order(s)	41st Division Administrative Instruction No. 20 issued in connection with 41st Division Operation Order No. 234 dated 31/3/18	31/03/1918	31/03/1918
Operation(al) Order(s)	41st Division Administrative Instruction No. 20 Issued In Connection With 41st Divisional Operation Order No. 233 Dated 29th March 1918	29/03/1918	29/03/1918
Miscellaneous	Appendix "A"		
Operation(al) Order(s)	41st Divisional Administrative Instruction No. 19 Issued In Connection With 41st. Divisional Operation Order No. 233 Dated 29th. March 1918	29/03/1918	29/03/1918
Miscellaneous	Appendix "A"		
Miscellaneous	41st Divisional Administrative Instruction No. 18 Dated 20th March 1918. Issued In Connection With 41st Division Order No. 226 of 20th. March 1918, And With Reference To 41st Divisional Administrative Instruction No. 16 Dated 19th March 1918.	20/03/1918	20/03/1918
Miscellaneous	Entraining Table Issued With 41st Division Administrative Instruction No. 18		
Miscellaneous	Appendix "A".		
Miscellaneous	41st Division Administrative Instruction No. 14 (Issued in continuation of 41st Division Order No. 224 dated 9/3/18)	09/03/1918	09/03/1918
Miscellaneous	Entraining Table to accompany 41st Division Administrative Instruction No. 14 dated March 9th 1918.	09/03/1918	09/03/1918
Miscellaneous	41st Divn Instn No. 12	26/02/1918	26/02/1918
War Diary	XIV Corps Administrative Instruction No. 33	25/02/1918	25/02/1918
Miscellaneous	Proforma-Vide Para. 6		
Miscellaneous	Distribution List. 41st Division Administrative Instruction No. 12		
Miscellaneous	41st Division No. Q/46/3/166 Lorry Details For Move.	25/02/1918	25/02/1918
Miscellaneous	41st Division No. Q.45/4/432	17/03/1918	17/03/1918
Miscellaneous	Amendment To 41st Divisional Administrative Instruction No. 15 Dated 17th March 1918	17/03/1918	17/03/1918
Miscellaneous	41st Division Administrative Instruction No. 15	17/03/1918	17/03/1918
Heading	A. & Q. 41st Division. April 1918 Appendices attached		
War Diary	St. Amand.	03/04/1918	03/04/1918
War Diary	Steenvoorde.	04/04/1918	04/04/1918
War Diary	Ypres.	09/04/1918	09/04/1918
War Diary	Vlamertinghe.	13/04/1918	26/04/1918
Miscellaneous	41st Division Administrative Instruction No. 21. Appendix I.	01/04/1918	01/04/1918

Type	Description	Date From	Date To
Miscellaneous	Table. "B". Embussing Programme.		
Miscellaneous	Table "A"		
Miscellaneous	41st Division Administrative Instruction No 25. issued in connection with 41st Division Operation Order No. 239 dated 7/4/18. Appendix 2	07/04/1918	07/04/1918
Miscellaneous	Location Table Issued In Continuation Of 41st Division Administrative Instruction No. 25 dated April 7th 1918	07/04/1918	07/04/1918
Miscellaneous	Personnel Of 29th. Division Will Be Relieved As Under.	07/04/1918	07/04/1918
Miscellaneous	41st Division Administrative Instruction No. 30. reference 41st Division Order No 245. dated 26/4/18. Appendix 3	26/04/1918	26/04/1918
Miscellaneous	41st. Division. Statement Showing Casualties For Month Of April 1918. Appendix 4		
Miscellaneous	41st. Division. Courts Martial Statement. April 1918. Appendix 5		
Heading	War Diary Of 41st. Division, "Q" Branch. From May 1st. 1916. To, May 31st. 1916 (Volume. 1.) 41 A & Q		
War Diary	Aldershot	01/05/1916	01/05/1916
War Diary	Menis	04/05/1916	09/05/1916
War Diary	La Lovie, Belgium.	09/05/1916	31/05/1916
War Diary	Steenwerck	30/05/1916	31/05/1916
Miscellaneous	41st Division Administrative Instruction No. 31. Issued In Connection With 41st Division Order No. 248 Dated 9th May 1918. Appendix A	09/05/1918	09/05/1918
Miscellaneous	41st. Division. Statement Showing Courts Martial For The Month Of May 1918. Appendix "B"		
Miscellaneous	41st. Division. Statement Showing Casualties And Sick Wastage For The Month Of May 1918. Appendix C		
Miscellaneous	41st. Division. Statement Showing Courts Martial For The Month Of May 1918. Appendix "B"		
Miscellaneous	41st. Division. Statement Showing Casualties And Sick Wastage For The Month Of May 1918. Appendix C		
Miscellaneous	41st Division. Daily Casualties. May 1916. Officers.		
Miscellaneous	41st Division. Daily Casualties. May 1916. Other Ranks.		
Miscellaneous	41st Division. Daily Sick Wastage. May 1916. Other Ranks.		
Heading	War Diary of A.A. & Q.M.G., 41st. Division. From 1/6/16 to 30/6/16. (Volume 2).		
War Diary	Lovie Chateau.	03/06/1918	03/06/1918
War Diary	Nieurlet	09/06/1918	09/06/1918
War Diary	Eperlecques.	24/06/1918	30/06/1918
War Diary	Steenwerck		
Miscellaneous	41st Division Administrative Instruction No. 32 reference 41st Division Operation Order No. 252 dated 1st June 1918 Appendix "A"	01/06/1918	01/06/1918
Miscellaneous	Table Of Light Railway Trains.		
Miscellaneous	March Table Of Transport.		
Miscellaneous	Further Administrative Instructions in continuation of 41st Division Administrative Instruction No. 32 dated June 1st 1918. Appendix "B"	01/06/1918	01/06/1918
Miscellaneous	Schedule "A"		
Miscellaneous	41st Division. Schedule "B".		
Miscellaneous	Billeting Schedule in connection with 41st Division Administrative Instruction No. 32 dated 1/6/18	01/06/1918	01/06/1918

Type	Description	Date From	Date To
Miscellaneous	41st Division Administrative Instruction No. 34 issued in connection with 41st Division Order No. 256 dated 25/6/18. Appendix C	25/06/1918	25/06/1918
Miscellaneous	41st Division Administrative Instruction No. 33 issued in connection with 41st Division Order No. 255 dated 24/6/18.	24/06/1918	24/06/1918
Operation(al) Order(s)	Addition to 41st Divl Administrative Order No. 33 dated 24/6/18	24/06/1918	24/06/1918
Miscellaneous	41st Division Administrative Instruction No. 35 issued in connection with 41st Division Order No. 257 dated 27th June 1918. Appendix "D"	27/06/1918	27/06/1918
Miscellaneous	Table "A"		
Miscellaneous	Ammunition To Be Held By 41st Division. Schedule "B"		
Miscellaneous	1st. Amendment To 41st. Division Administrative Instruction No. 35 dated June 28th 1918.	28/06/1918	28/06/1918
Miscellaneous	Statement Of Courts Martial For June, 1918. Appendix E		
Miscellaneous	41st. Division. Casualties And Sick. June 1918. Appendix F		
War Diary	La Linge.	03/07/1918	03/07/1918
War Diary	K.24.c.2.3. Sheet 27.	23/07/1918	23/07/1918
Miscellaneous	41st Division Administrative Instruction No. 36 issued in connection with 41st Division G/371/29/5 dated 23/7/18 and G. 421/29/5 dated 24/7/18. Appendix "A"	23/07/1918	23/07/1918
Miscellaneous	41st Division Administrative Instruction No. 36 issued in connection with 41st Division G/371/29/5 dated 23/7/18 and G. 421/29/5 dated 24/7/18.	23/07/1918	23/07/1918
Miscellaneous	Addendum To 41st Division Administrative Instruction No. 36 Issued In Connection With 41st Division G371/29/5 Dated 23/7/18 And G421/29/5 Dated 24/7/18	23/07/1918	23/07/1918
Miscellaneous	41st. Division. Casualty And Sick. July 1918. Appendix "B"		
Miscellaneous	Statement Of Courts Martial For July 1918. Appendix C		
War Diary	K.24.c.2.3.	27/08/1918	30/08/1918
Miscellaneous	41st. Division. Casualties And Sick Evacuations-August 1918.		
Miscellaneous	41st. Division. Courts Martial For The Month Of August 1918.		
Miscellaneous	Amendment To 41st. Divisional Administrative Instruction No. 40 Dated 27th. August 1918. Table 'D'.	27/08/1918	27/08/1918
Miscellaneous	41st Division Administrative Instruction No. 40 issued in connection with 41st Division Order No. 266 dated August 27th 1918.	27/08/1918	27/08/1918
Miscellaneous	Schedule A. (1). (Broad Guage).		
Miscellaneous	Schedule "A2" Light Railways.		
Miscellaneous	Schedule A.3. Busses.		
Miscellaneous	Table "B" For Transport. (Ref Sheet 27)		
Miscellaneous	Sheet 2. (March Table).		
Miscellaneous	Table "C".		
Miscellaneous	Table "D" Accommodation.		

WO95/2620
41 Div A&Q
Mar '18 – July '18

②

41 DIV

A & Q BRANCH

MAR 1918 — JULY

FROM ITALY

Army Form C. 2118.

WAR DIARY
or
INTELLIGENCE SUMMARY.

(Erase heading not required.)

"A" and "Q" Branch.
41st. Division.

March 1918.

Place	Date	Hour	Summary of Events and Information	Remarks and references to Appendices
Italy.	2/3/18.		Divisional Headquarters entrained CAMPOSAMPIERO (Italy) detraining MONDICOURT (France) March 7th 1918 - Divisional Headquarters established at COUTURELLE.	1.
France.	10/3/18.		Divisional Headquarters moved to LUCHEUX. Reorganisation of Division to 3 battalions per Brigade and a Divisional Machine Gun Battalion took place. - Completed March 20th.	2. 3.
	20/3/18.		Divisional Headquarters moved to BAIZIEUX prior to moving into line.	
	22nd - 28th Mch.		Division moved into action and Headquarters established at FAVREUIL, later moving back to GREVILLERS, - ACHIET le PETIT, - BUCQUOY, - SOUASTRE, - BAILLEULVILLE, - ST.AMAND.	4. 5.
			A list of Casualties is attached.	6.
			A statement of Courts Martial is attached.	
	26/4/18.			

Lieut.Colonel,
A.A.&.Q.M.G.,
41st.Division.

41st DIVISION.

COURT MARTIAL STATEMENT FOR MONTH OF MARCH, 1918.

UNIT.	No. of cases.	Charge.	Sentence.
12th E.Surrey Regt.	2.	Drunkenness.	(1) 21 days F.P.1. (1) 14 days F.P.1.
18th K.R.R.Corps.	6.	(5) Drunkenness. (1) Breach of censorship.	(4) 14 days F.P.1. Fined £1 (1) 28 days F.P.1. Fined £1 42 days F.P.2.
11th R.W.Kent Regt.	2.	(1) Absent without leave. (1) Drunkenness.	Reduced to Corporal. 21 days F.P.1. Fined £1
20th Durham L.I.	2.	Drunkenness.	(1) Reduced to ranks. (1) Reduced to Cpl.
23rd Middlesex Regt.	1.	Drunkenness.	28 days F.P.1.
11th Queen's.	1.	Neglecting to obey G.R.O.	28 days F.P.1.
10th R.W.Kent Regt.	2.	(1) Drunkenness. (1) Conduct to prejudice of good order & military discipline.	28 days F.P.1. Fined £1 90 days F.P.1.
26th R.Fusiliers.	1.	Absent without leave.	2 years I.H.L.
32nd R.Fusiliers.	2.	Drunkenness.	(1) 21 days F.P.1. Fined 10/- (1) 90 days F.P.1.
21st K.R.R.Corps.	1.	(a) Insubordinate language to superior officer. (b) Drunkenness. (c) Escaping arrest.	90 days F.P.1.
Z/41 T.M.Bty.	1.	Drunkenness.	Reduced to ranks.
138th.Field Ambce.	1.	Conduct to prejudice of good order and mil.Discp.	28t days F.P.1.
A/187th.Bde.R.F.A.	1.	Striking senior officer.	2 years I.H.L.
19th.Middlesex Regt.	2.	(a) Neglect of duty. (b) Drunkenness.	21 Days F.P.1. Reduced to Ranks.
233rd.Field Coy.R.E.	2.	(a) Neglect of duty. (b) Neglect to obey postal instructions. Conduct to prejudice of good order and mil.Discp.	Reduced to ranks. (Quashed). 3 years. P.S.

Appendix 6.

FULL LIST OF ACTUAL CASUALTIES FOR PERIOD 21st MARCH to 1st APRIL, 1918.

UNIT.	Officers.			Other Ranks.		
	Killed	Wounded	Missing	Killed	Wounded	Missing
122nd Infantry Bde.						
12th E.Surrey Regt.	2	6	4	7	46	186
15th Hampshire Regt.	-	3	-	16	61	6
18th K.R.R.Corps.	1	5	9	7	70	412
Trench Mortar Bty.	-	-	-	-	4	12
123rd Infantry Bde.						
11th Queen's.	1	5	8	12	-	361
10th R.W.Kent Rgt.	-	2	12	14	29	408
23rd Middlesex.	4	5	5	43	172	123
Trench Mortar Bty.	-	-	-	-	-	-
124th Infantry Bde.						
10th Queen's.	1	15	4	33	184	148
26th R.Fusiliers.	2	18	2	39	124	127
20th Durham L.I.	2	10	2	47	221	48
Trench Mortar Bty.	-	-	-	-	-	-
Pioneers.						
19th Middlesex.	1	3	2	7	60	85
Machine Gun Corps.						
41st Bn.	3	2	2	13	64	63
Royal Engineers.						
228 Field Coy.	1	1	-	1	14	8
233 do.	1	-	-	-	5	1
237 do.	-	-	-	1	13	2
R.A.M.C.						
138 Field Amb.	-	-	-	-	7	-
139 do.	-	2	-	5	9	17
140 do.	-	-	-	5	7	2
Medical Officers.	-	2	2	-	-	-
41 Div Train.	-	-	-	-	1	-
238 Emplyt. Coy.	-	-	-	-	1	-
41 Div Signal Coy.	1	-	-	-	4	1
Royal Artillery.						
187 Brigade.	2	4	-	2	38	-
190 Brigade.	1	1	-	4	33	3
D.A.C.	-	-	-	-	-	-
TOTAL.	21	84	52	256	1167	2011

41st DIVISION ADMINISTRATIVE INSTRUCTION No. 20
issued in connection with 41st Division
Operation Order No.234 dated 31/3/18.

1. Troops on relief from the line will be accommodated for the night 1st/2nd and 2nd/3rd as follows, and not as shown in Operation Order No.234 :-

   Divisional H.Qtrs.   HENU or ST.AMAND.
   122nd Inf.Bde Group.   MARIEUX aerodrome. I.19.a.
   123rd Inf.Bde Group.   THIEVRES
   124th Inf.Bde Group.   FAMECHON
   Pioneers.   PAS.
   Machine G.Bn.   PAS.
   H.Q.Div Train.   PAS.
   52nd M.V.Section.   PAS.
   S.A.A.Sec.D.A.C.   FAMECHON.(Bivouacs).

   Billeting parties will meet D.A.A.G. on 1st instant as follows :-
       Church PAS 2.p.m.
       Church FAMECHON 3.p.m.
       Church THIEVRES 4.p.m.
       Church MARIEUX 5.p.m.

2. 40 lorries to convey such troops as are tired and unable to march will be provided, to be on BIENVILLERS - SOUASTRE Road, head at D.18.central facing West.

Serial No.	Units.	Time of embussment.	Place of debussment.
1.	122 Inf.Bde. 1 Co.M.G.Bn.	11p.m. 1st.	I.8.c. east of THIEVRES.
2.	123 Inf.Bde. 1 Co.M.G.Bn.	3.a.m. 2nd.	I.8.c. east of THIEVRES.
3.	124 Inf.Bde. 2 Cos.M.G.Bn.	7.a.m. 2nd.	C.26.b. FAMECHON.

   Troops embussing will be formed up on the North side and clear of the roads 10 minutes before scheduled time of embussment. Each serial No. will take 1200 men only, so that any men who are fit to march will be formed into a party, and despatched by march route.

3. Transport of troops moving in serial numbers 1, 2, and 3 will move to new billeting area on night 1st/2nd except cookers of serial No.3 which will proceed to embussing point so as to serve tea etc two hours before embussment. Transport of R.E.Companies and Field Ambulances will move independently to new area to reach there by 12 noon 2nd.

/4.

4. Divisional Train, 52nd Mobile Veterinary Section will move to new area on the evening of 1st April.

5. B.A.A Section of Divisional Ammunition Column will move to new area on morning of 2nd April to be in there by 12 noon.

All ammunition echelons will march full.

6. Trench shelters, ammunition, petrol tins, and stores now in the MOGUOY Line and the Divisional Dump at BESARTS will be handed over on relief.

7. Refilling points 2nd April will be in Brigade Areas to be selected by Officer Commanding Train and notified to all concerned.

Lieut Colonel,
A.A. & Q.M.G.
41st Division.

March 31st 1918.

Copies to :-

122nd Inf.Brigade.
123rd Inf.Brigade.
124th Inf.Brigade.
122nd Inf.Bde Trans Offr.
123rd   "   "   "   "
124th   "   "   "   "
19th Middlesex
  " do - Tran.Offr.
Div M.Gun Bn.
   do - Tran Offr.
C.R.E.
Div Train.
52nd Mob.Section.
D.A.D.V.S.
Camp Commandant.
A.D.M.S.
D.A.D.O.S.
A.P.M.
"G"
Pents.

War Diary.
File.
4th Corps Q.
52nd Divn Q.
41st M.T.Company.
B.A.A.Section D.A.C.
O.R.A. (for A.P.M.)
41st Signal Co.

41st. DIVISIONAL ADMINISTRATIVE INSTRUCTION
No. 19 ISSUED IN CONNECTION WITH 41st. DIVISIONAL
OPERATION ORDER No. 233 DATED 29th. MARCH 1918.

1. **AMMUNITION SUPPLY.**

   Railhead.   MONDICOURT.

   S.A.A. Section D.A.C.   COUIN.

   Divisional Dump.   ESSART F.19.a.4.5.
   (contents see appendix 'A').

2. **SUPPLIES.**

   Divisional Train.   AUTHIE.

   'F' Echelon 1st
   Line Transport.   COUIN.

   WATER.

   The water supply in BUCQUOY is not good. There are several wells of moderate quality. Water carts should be sent up, and Brigades now in the Line have been told to hand over a proportion of their petrol tins. Wells exist at,

   L.3.a.6.3.
   L.3.a.5.0.
   L.3.a.8.6.

3. **ORDNANCE.**

   D.A.D.O.S. office is at St. AMAND.

4. **MEDICAL.**

   Collecting posts.   -   F.27.b.5.5.
                                 F.13.b.9.5.
                                 F.19.a.5.1.

   A.D.S. BIENVILLERS. L.2.d.6.7.
   M.D.S. AUTHIE.

5. **R.E.**

   Small dumps exist at E.10.c.1.3. and E.24.b.7.5., an additional dump is being formed at E.9.a.2.9.

6. **PROVOST INSTRUCTIONS.**

   (a). Stragglers posts will be established at,

   F.19.c.6.3.
   F.14.c.9.1.
   E.6.a.6.0.

   (b). Traffic posts will be taken over by A.P.M. under arrangements with A.P.M. 42nd Division.

   Lieut. Colonel,
   A.A. & Q.M.G.,
   41st. Division.

29/3/18.

APPENDIX "A".

Contents of Divisional Dump ESSART.

    S.A.A. — 600,000 rounds.

    Stokes Ammunition. — 1,700 rounds with ballistite rings.

    Rifle Grenades, No.23.

    Very Lights, 1" Illuminating.

Copies to all recipients of 41st Division Operation Order No.857, and Brigade Transport Officers.

41st. DIVISIONAL ADMINISTRATIVE INSTRUCTION
No. 19 ISSUED IN CONNECTION WITH 41st. DIVISIONAL
OPERATION ORDER No. 233 DATED 29th. MARCH 1918.

1. **AMMUNITION SUPPLY.**

    Railhead.   MONDICOURT.

    S.A.A. Section D.A.C.   COUIN.

    Divisional Dump.   ESSART F.19.a.4.5.
    (contents see appendix 'A').

2. **SUPPLIES.**

    Divisional Train.   AUTHIE.

    'F' Echelon 1st
    Line Transport.   COUIN.

    WATER.

    The water supply in BUCQUOY is not good. There are several wells of moderate quality. Water carts should be sent up, and Brigades now in the Line have been told to hand over a proportion of their petrol tins. Wells exist at,

    L.3.a.6.3.
    L.3.a.5.0.
    L.3.a.8.6.

3. **ORDNANCE.**

    D.A.D.O.S. office is at ST.AMAND.

4. **MEDICAL.**

    Collecting posts. -   F.27.b.5.5.
                             F.13.b.9.5.
                             F.19.a.5.1.

    A.D.S. BIENVILLERS.   L.2.d.6.7.
    M.D.S. AUTHIE.

5. **R.E.**

    Small dumps exist at E.10.c.1.3. and E.24.b.7.5., an additional dump is being formed at E.9.a.2.9.

6. **PROVOST INSTRUCTIONS.**

    (a). Stragglers posts will be established at,

    F.19.c.6.3.
    F.14.c.9.1.
    E.6.a.6.0.

    (b). Traffic posts will be taken over by A.P.M. under arrangements with A.P.M. 42nd Division.

29/3/18.

Lieut. Colonel,
A.A. & Q.M.G.,
41st. Division.

APPENDIX "A".

Contents of Divisional Dump ESSART.

    S.A.A.   -   600,000 rounds.

    Stokes Ammunition. -   1,700 rounds with ballistite rings.

    Rifle Grenades, No.23.

    Very Lights, 1" Illuminating.

Copies to all recipients of 41st Division Operation Order No.233, and Brigade Transport Officers.

SECRET.   War Diary   3.

41st. DIVISIONAL ADMINISTRATIVE INSTRUCTION NO.18
DATED 20th MARCH 1918.
ISSUED IN CONNECTION WITH 41st.DIVISION ORDER NO.226 of 20th.March 1918, AND WITH REFERENCE TO 41st DIVISIONAL ADMINISTRATIVE INSTRUCTION No.16 DATED 19th MAY 1918.

1. Troops and Transport will entrain in accordance with attached table.

2. Transport will report at the Station 3 Hours and personnel 1 Hour before the advertised time of departure of the trains.

3. Each Brigade will detail a party of 2 Officers and 100 men to lhead the Transport Trains and those parties will report 3 Hours before the departure of the train, and will proceed on the train they load.

4. Trains will be composed as follows.

Personnel. (T.T. or T.T.P).   ) (2 Brake Vans.
   2 Brake Vans.   ) (
  44 Third Class Coaches.   ) (48 Covered Trucks.
   2 First Class Coaches.   or) (
   2 Covered Goods Wagons.   ) (
   (For Lewis Guns and Handcarts)   ) (
   (less transport.   ) (

No vehicles or horses may be carried in these trains.

Transport.

   1 Passenger coach.
  30 Covered Wagons.
  17 Flats each carrying 4 axles - one truck on each train must carry 5 axles.
   2 Brake Vans (For Railway personnel only).

5. Billeting parties with bicycles will be sent on the first train of each Brigade Group.

6. The O.C. of each train will bring with him a State in duplicate showing strength in personnel and numbers of animals and axles.

7. No troops will enter the station yard until the O.C. has reported to the R.T.O. and handed him one copy of his state.

8. The A.P.M. will detail one N.C.O. and 3 police to report at each station 30 minutes before entrainment begins.

9. Breast ropes for horses must be provided by Units.

10. The entrainment will be directed by the D.A.Q.M.G. The following are appointed Entraining Officers.

   at MONDICOURT   Captain A.H.REID.
   at SAULTY.   Captain H.A.B.QUARE.

These Officers will report completion of move by wire to Divisional Headquarters as soon as the last train has left, by wire.

11. Detrainment will be directed by A.A.&.Q.M.G..
    The following are appointed Detraining Officers :-

    ALBERT   Lt.Hogg M.C.
    EDGE HILL. Captain Shone.

12. Instructions re lorries will be issued later.

13. ACKNOWLEDGE.

                                    Lieut Colonel,
                                    A.A. & Q.M.G.
March 20th 1918.   41st Division.

Copies to all recipients of 41st Divl Administrative
Instruction No.16 dated March 19th 1918.

ENTRAINING TABLE ISSUED WITH 41st DIVISION ADMINISTRATIVE INSTRUCTION No. 18.

122nd Brigade.

Unit.	Entraining Station.	Time of Departure.	Detraining Station	
Bde.H.Q. personnel. T.M.Battery. 122th Fld Amb. personnel. H.Q.&.1.Company of Machine Gun Battalion. "A". Battalion.	MONDICOURT.	5.0.p.m.	EDGE HILL	T.T.
"B" & "C" Battalions.	MONDICOURT	6.0.p.m.	EDGE HILL	T.T
As in Appendix "A".	SAULTY	8.30.p.m.	EDGE HILL	T.O.

123rd Brigade.

Bde H.Q. personnel. T.M.Bty. 136th Fld Art personnel. 1 Co. & 2 Sections M.G.Bn. 23rd Essex Regt.	MONDICOURT	9.a.m.	ALBERT	T.T.
11th Bn.Queen's. 10th R.W.Kents. Divl H.Q. personnel.	MONDICOURT	11.a.m.	ALBERT	T.T.
As shown in Appendix "A".	MONDICOURT	12 noon	EDGE HILL	T.O.

124th Brigade.

As shown in Appendix "A".	SAULTY.	2.30.p.m	ALBERT	T.O.
20th D.L.I. Personnel Bde H.Q., T.M.B. 140th Fld Amb personnel. 1 Co 2 Sections M.G.Bn.	SAULTY	4.30.p.m	ALBERT	T.T.
10th Queen's & 26th R.Fsilrs.	SAULTY	5.30 p.m	ALBERT	T.T.

APPENDIX "A".
==*=*=*=*=*=*=*=*

	Personnel.	Axles.	Horses.
Bde H.Qtrs & 1 L.GS. Wagon and team.	20.	2.	9.
Signal Section.	28.	2.	9.
From each Battln. @ 4. G.S.L.Wagons.	12.	24.	24.
" " " @ 2. Water Carts.	12.	6.	6.
" " " @ 1. Mess Cart.	3.	3.	3.
" " " @ 2. Travelling Kitchens.	6.	12.	12.
" " " @ 1. Maltese Cart.	3.	3.	3.
" " " @ 11 Riding Horses and 7 Pack.	54.	–	54.
From M.Gun (on each of three trains :– 6.G.S.L.Wagons.	10.	12	20.
Battalion (on each of two trains. :– 1 Water Cart.	1.	1.	2.
(on one train :– 1 Mess Cart.	1.	1.	1.
:– Riding Horses.	8.	0.	8.
From Fld Ambulance. 2. G.S.L. wagons.	2.	4.	4.
" " 4 Riding Horses.	4.	0.	4.
Loading Party.	101.	–	–

41st Division Administrative Instruction No. 14.
(Issued in continuation of 41st Division Order No.224 dated 9/3/18).

1. With reference to 41st Division Order No. 224 of 9th March.

2. The Division will entrain in accordance with the attached table. Times of departure of the trains will be notified later.

3. Transport will report at entraining stations three hours and personnel one hour before the scheduled time of departure of the respective trains.

4. Each train will consist of the following vehicles :-
   30 Covered trucks.
   17 Flat Trucks.
   1 Officers coach.

5. The Officer Commanding 19th Middlesex (Pioneers) will detail one platoon to help load trains Nos. 35 and 38, one platoon to help load train No.36 and one platoon to help load train No. 37.
   These platoons will report at the entraining stations three hours before the time of departure of trains Nos 35, 36 and 37 respectively, and will entrain on trains Nos 38, 36, and 37 respectively.

6. Units will entrain with the unexpired portion of the days rations plus rations for the day subsequent to entrainment on the man. The Officer Commanding Divisional Train will arrange on receipt of a warning wire from this office, to load supply vehicles from Supply Column in sufficient time for the supply wagons to entrain full.

7. Baggage and supply wagons will entrain with the units to which they are allotted.
   Baggage wagons will join units on receipt of warning wire.
   Supply wagons will join units as soon as they are loaded with the rations for the second day subsequent to entrainment, (vide para.6.) or, in case of lack of time, will proceed direct to the entraining station.

8. ACKNOWLEDGE.

March 9th 1918.

Major,
D.A.Q.M.G.
41st Division.

Copies to all units and D.A.D.R.T.

Entraining Table to accompany 41st Division Administrative Instruction No. 14 dated March 9th 1918.

ENTRAINING STATIONS.

Serial No.	CONDICOURT. Units.	Train No.	DOULLENS NORTH. Units.	Train No.	DOULLENS SOUTH. Units.
1.	122 Inf.B.Q., 2de Sig.Sec., 122 .G.Co., 122 T..., 1 Coy. 1 Cooker and team of 12th E.Surrey Regt.	2.	123 Bde H.Q., Bde Sig S/c., 123 .G.C., 123 T..., 1 Coy. 1 Cooker and team of 11th Queens.	3.	124 Bde H.Q., Bde Sig Sec., 124 .G.Co., 124 T..., 1 Coy. 1 Cooker and team of 10th Queens.
4.	12th E.Surreys less 1 Coy, 1 Cooker, 1 Cooker and team.	5.	11th Queen's less 1 Coy, 1 Cooker and team.	6.	10th Queen's less 1 Coy, 1 Cooker and team.
7.	11th R.W.Kents less 1 Coy, 1 Cooker and team.	8.	10th R.W.Kents less 1 Coy, 1 Cooker and team.	9.	26th R.Fusiliers less 1 Coy, 1 Cooker and team.
10.	15th Hants less 1 Coy, 1 Cooker and team.	11.	23rd Middlesex Regt. less 1 Coy, 1 Cooker and team.	12.	32nd R.Fusiliers less 1 Coy, 1 Cooker and team.
13.	18th K.R.R.C. less 1 Coy, 1 Cooker and team.	14.	20th D.L.I. less 1 Coy, 1 Cooker and team.	15.	21st K.R.R.C. less 1 Coy, 1 Cooker and team.
16.	Divl H.Qrs., H.Qrs Sig.Sec Sig Co., H.Q.Divl A...	17.	1 Coy 1 Cooker & Team of 10th R.W.Kents., No. 3 Coy. Divl Train, 233 Field Co.R.E.	18.	100 M.Gun Co., Divl Employ Company, 1 Coy. 1 Cooker and team of 26th R.Fusiliers, H.Qtrs Divl Artillery.

Entraining Table (Sheet 2).

Train No.	ORDIGOURT. Units.	Train No.	DOULLENS NORTH Units.	Train No.	DOULLENS SOUTH. Units.
19.	1 Coy, 1 Cooker and team of 11th R.West Kent Regt. No.2 Coy Div Train. 229th Field Co. R.E.	20.	1 Coy, 1 Cooker and team of 23rd Middlesex. 1 Coy, 1 Cooker and team of 20th D.L.I. 139th Field Ambulance. Mobile Vet Section.	21.	1 Coy, 1 Cooker and team of 19th Middlesex. No.4 Coy. Div Train. No 237th Field Co. R.E.
22.	1 Coy, 1 Cooker and team of 15th Hants. 1 Coy, 1 Cooker and team of 16th K.R.R.C. 138th Field Ambulance Co. H.Qtrs Div Train.	23.	19th Middlesex Regt less 1 Coy, and 3 platoons, 1 Cooker and team.	24.	1 Coy, 1 Cooker and team of 32nd R.Fusiliers. 1 Coy, 1 Cooker and team of 21st K.R.R.C. 140th Field Ambulance.
25.	A/190 Bde R.F.A. 1 G.S.wagon and 4 limt. amm wagons and teams of No.1 Sec. D.A.C.	26.	B/190 Bde R.F.A. 1 G.S.wagon and 4 limt Amm wagons and teams of No.1 Sec. D.A.C.	27.	190th Bde R.F.A. H.Qtrs No 1 Sect. D.A.C. less 4 G.S. wagons and 16 limt. amm. wagons and teams.
28.	C/190 Bde R.F.A. 1 G.S.wagon and 4 limt. Amm wagons and teams of No.1 Sect D.A.C.	29.	D/190 Bde R.F.A. 1 G.S.wagon and 4 limt amm wagons of No. 1 Section D.A.C. and teams	30.	A/190th Bde R.F.A. 1 G.S.wagon and 4 limt. amm wagons and teams of No.2 Sec D.A.C.
31.	B/190th Bde R.F.A. 1 G.S.wagon and 4 limt. amm wagons and teams of No.2 Section D.A.C.	32.	190th Bde H.Qtrs R.F.A. No.2 Section D.A.C. less 4 G.S. wagons and 16 limt. amm. wagons and teams.	33.	C/190th Bde R.F.A. 1 G.S.wagon and 4 limt amm wagons and teams of No. 2 Section D.A.C.

Entraining Table. (Page 3).

CANDICOURT.		DOULLENS NORTH.		DOULLENS SOUTH.	
Train No.	Units.	Train No.	Units.	Train No.	Units.
34.	D/190 Bde R.F.A.. 1 G.S.wagon and 4 limt arm'd wagons and teams of No. 2 Section D.A.C.	35.	H.Q.D.A.C. H.Q. Coy Div Train.	36.	One third "B" Echelon D.A.C. X Trench M.Btty. 1 Platoon 19th Middlesex.
37.	One third "A" Echelon D.A.C. Y.Trench Btty. 1 Platoon 19th Middlesex.	38.	One third "A" Echelon D.A.C. 1 Platoon 19th Middlesex.		

S E C R E T.

41st Divn Instn No. 12.

Reference 41st Division Order No. 222 and G.H.Q. instructions Q.M.G. No. Q.C/24 (circulated herewith).

1. The 41st Division less Artillery) will entrain at the following stations in accordance with train tables which will be issued later. (Table attached)
   POJANA
   FONTANIVA
   CARMIGNANA.
   PADOVA C.M.
   CAMPOSAMPIERO.

2. Major E.S.White, D.A.Q.M.G., 41st Division will be in charge of the entrainment with Headquarters c/o D.A.D.R.T. CAMPOSAMPIERO.
   Entraining Officers at stations will be as follows :-
   Capt A.H.REID   CAMPOSAMPIERO.
   Lieut S.R.HOGG, M.C. POJANA.
   Lt.MUMMERY.   FONTANIVA.
   Lt.BENNETT.   CARMIGNANA.
   Capt SHONE.   PADOVA C.M.
   These Officers will entrain on the last train from their respective stations.
   Entraining Officers will telephone to the D.A.Q.M.G. as soon after noon as possible each day giving strengths in Officers, other ranks, and horses by types, and vehicles by types entrained for the 24 hours up to noon on the day of reporting.
   O.C.Signal Company will detail two despatch riders to be at disposal of the Staff Officer supervising entrainment.

3. C.R.E. will detail a Section R.E. to each entraining station as directed by Q.M.G. No. Q.C/24.

4. Personnel will report at entraining station one hour and transport three hours before advertised time of departure of train.
   A loading party of 3 Officers and 100 other ranks in addition to Transport personnel will be detailed to proceed with the Transport. In cases where several small units proceed by same train the Brigade concerned will detail a special party to assist.
   123rd Infantry Brigade will detail a party of one Officer and 50 other ranks to load train No. 5, to be at CAMPOSAMPIERO Station 3 hours before scheduled time of departure.

5. Reference para. 3 (a) Q.M.G's Q.C/24 seven days rations will be delivered and issued at the entraining stations, except FONTANIVA, under arrangements to be made by G.H.Q. XIVth Corps are transferring rations which will be dumped at CARMIGNANA for FONTANIVA, to FONTANIVA. O.C.Train will arrange to take over these rations. He will detail one Officer and sufficient issuers at FONTANIVA Station to be at FONTANIVA Station by 12 noon 28th. G.H.Q. are providing Officers and issuers for the other Entraining stations.

Sheet 2.

Sheet 2.

5.   These rations will be issued daily as required
(continued) to units on presentation of their indents. Separate indents
must be rendered for the seven days rations to be put on the
train and the one day which is to be packed in the
supply wagons.

Two days bread for 100% of strength will be issued
before entrainment. Only 5 days biscuits will therefore
be put on the train.

Units will have these indents ready to hand over to
Supply Officers at Entraining Station 3 hours before
departure of train.

Supply and Baggage wagons will be sent to units
by 5.p.m. on the day previous to Entrainment and will
entrain with the units to which they are allotted. Supply
wagons will carry one day's supplies.

6.   A State and certificate on pro-forma attached, will
be handed to the Officer superintending entrainment at the
station.

7.   Group billeting parties will travel on the first train
for each group.

8.   Harness and saddlery will be taken off before entrainment
and if possible placed in a truck other than that used for
horses. Complete sets of saddlery should be tied together
so that each set is kept separate and is readily available
on detrainment. Buckets will be taken in the truck
with the horses.

9.   The Senior Officer in each Train will be O.C.Train.
He will be responsible for the discipline of the
troops on his train, and that the wishes of the Railway
authorities are carried out.

No men are permitted to travel on open trucks, or
the top of carriages. Men are to be specially warned
regarding the danger of the electrified portion of the
line. Once personnel are entrained no man will leave
his carriage or truck except with the permission of an
Officer.

In order to prevent men being left behind at haltes,
when men are permitted to alight a bugle should be sounded
five minutes before departure of train.

In cases where there is no R.T.O. it is suggested
that liaison be established with the engine driver.

Latrine accommodation provided is to be used and
indiscriminate fouling of the ground to be avoided as far
as possible.

At Haltes, Regimental Police should patrol the train.
All possible precautions must be taken to prevent
an outbreak of fire, and fire orders will be issued by
Officers Commanding Trains.

10.   Units are reminded that lights are not provided
in first or third class carriages and only one lantern
per covered truck.

11.   No oats will be fed for the first 24 hours of the
journey and after that half feeds only.

12.   The Foden Lorry will entrain with Serial No. 4196
under orders of O.C.Divisional M.T.Company.

13.   Instructions regarding Medical arrangements are
attached.

Lieut Col,

SECRET.　　　XIV CORPS ADMINISTRATIVE INSTRUCTION NO.33.
━━━
MEDICAL ARRANGEMENTS FOR TRAIN JOURNEYS.
═══

Divisions moving by rail will make the following Medical arrangements :-

FIRST AID. (1) (a) Each train will carry either a Regimental Medical Officer or 1 non-commissioned officer and 1 man R.A.M.C. from a Field Ambulance.

(b) Accommodation assigned to Medical and Sanitary Personnel will be marked with a red cross.

Cases of serious sudden illness. (2) Cases of very serious sudden illness which cannot be treated on the train will be handed over with written instructions to the French or Italian authorities at the first important station.
R.A.M.C. non-commissioned officer with trains will apply to Medical Officer of next train for assistance in cases they are unable to deal with.

Medical Equipment. (3) Each train will carry either the Regimental Medical equipment of a Unit, or surgical haversack, water bottle, two stretchers and 4 blankets.

Medical Comforts. (4) The following Medical comforts will be carried on each train :-
12 tins of milk.　12 tins of OXO.
1 lb. of tea.　2 lbs of sugar.
12 candles.

Sanitary Personnel. (5) A Sanitary Squad will be allotted to each train. The Regimental Sanitary Squads will be augmented as necessary.
The personnel of each train sanitary squad will be 1 N.C.O. and 8 men.

Sanitary Equipment. (6) Each Sanitary Squad will be provided with the following:-
2 Spades. 2 Shovels. 4 Brooms. 20 Sandbags.

Conservancy at Halts. (7) At all halts where Military Latrines do not exist, sanitary squads will prepare trench latrines and urinals.
These will be carefully filled in before departure.

Cleansing of carriages (8) At all fixed halts the railway vehicles will be vacated and swept out by the Sanitary Squad.

Receptacles for Refuse. (9) To expedite work of sanitary squads, one of the sandbags mentioned in para.6, will be placed in each covered vehicle, and used for reception of rubbish.

Spitting. (10) Spitting in all vehicles will be made the subject of disciplinary action.

Medical Arrangements (cont'd)

Entraining Medical Officers.

(11) Entraining Medical Officers will be detailed to supervise Medical arrangements for the entrainment, and proceed by the last train from each entraining station.

Detraining Medical Officers.

(12) Detraining Medical Officers will be detailed and these officers will proceed by first train without a Medical Officer from each of the entraining stations. They will be responsible for the collection of all medical equipment from trains without medical officers and ordnance equipment and medical comforts from all trains.
They will arrange for disposal of sick at detraining stations.

                    (Signed) H.L.ALEXANDER,
                           Brigadier General,
25/2/1918.   D.A.&Q.M.G., XIV CORPS.

PROFORMA.-VIDE PARA. 6.
✸✸

ENTRAINING STRENGTH.

HORSES.			HORSE DRAWN VEHICLES.		MECHANICAL VEHICLES.			
Officers.	O. R.	Riders.	H.D.	L.D.	4 Wheeled.	2 Wheeled.	Motorcars.	Motor Ambulances.	Lorries.	Steam Lorries.

I hereby certify that my Unit is complete in equipment, and in the Rations, Petrol &c. as laid down
in Q.W.G., G.H.Q. No. Q.C.24, and in 41st Divisional Instruction No. 12.

Commanding----------

DISTRIBUTION LIST.

	41st Division Administrative Instruction.No.12. No.of Copies.	Q.M.G.;Q.C./24. No.of copies.
122nd Infantry Brigade.	7.	1.
123rd Infantry Brigade.	7.	1.
124th Infantry Brigade.	7.	1.
C.R.E.	4.	1.
C.R.A.	1.	-
41st Divisional Train.	6.	1.
A.D.M.S.	4.	1.
File.	1.	1.
War Diary.	2.	-
Camp Commandant.	1.	1) To circulate
A.P.M.	1.	(to A.P.M.
D.A.D.O.S.	1.	) D.A.D.O.S.
D.A.D.V.S.	1.	(&
		) D.A.D.V.S.
41st Divl. M.T. Coy.	1.	1.
19th Middlesex.	1.	-
41st Divl. Signal Coy.	1.	-
199th Machine Gun Coy.	1.	-
238th Employment Coy.	1.	-
52nd Mobile Vety. Section.	1.	-
"G"	1.	-
Divl. Machine Gun Officer.	1.	-
Baths Officer.	1.	-
Lieutenant Hogg.	1.	-
Lieutenant Mummery.	1.	-
Captain Reid.	1.	-
Captain Shone.	1.	-
Divl. Gas Officer.	1.	-
D.A.Q.M.G.	1.	-
XlV Corps "Q"	1.	-
S.M.T.O.,XlV Corps.	1.	-
A.D.C. 1.	1.	-

※※※※※※※※※※※※※※※※

S E C R E T.　　　　　　　　　　　　41st Division No. Q/46/3/166.

122nd Infantry Brigade.　　　　Camp Commandant.
123rd Infantry Brigade.　　　　O.C. 238 Employment.Coy.
124th Infantry Brigade.　　　　D.A.D.O.S.
19th Middlesex Regt.　　　　　 O.C. Crumps.
199 Machine Gun Coy.　　　　　 O.C. Divnl. Train.
C. R. E.　　　　　　　　　　　 O.C. Signals.

LORRY DETAILS FOR MOVE.

Ten lorries for each Infantry Brigade will remain with Brigades until completion of the move, returning to Park on the night of February 27th- 1918.

An A.S.C. Officer will be in charge of each group.

In the case of the 123rd and 124th Brigades, the above mentioned officers will join their groups tonight with rations for the drivers.

Two lorries will report to 19th Middlesex Regt. at 7 a.m. Feby. 26th, as already arranged and will remain with the Regiment until the evening of the 27th inst.

Ten lorries will report to Camp Commandant at 7 a.m. 26th instant for move of Divisional Headquarters and will make at least two journeys to CAMPOSAMPIERO.

The Camp Commandant will deal with all applications for help in transport from C.R.E., O.C. Div. Train, O.C. Signal Coy., D.A.D.O.S. and O i/c Crumps. If necessary 'Crumps' kit must be left until the 27th instant.

The above amplifies and does not cancel the lorry detail issued under this office No. Q.46/3/122 dated Feb 23rd 1918.

Except for D.H.Q.

　　　　　　　　　　　　　　　　　　　　　　[signature]
　　　　　　　　　　　　　　　　　　　　　　Major,
25/2/18.　　　　　　　　　　　　　　　　　　D.A.Q.M.G., 41st Division.

SECRET. 41st Division No. Q.45/4/432.

12th E.Sussex Regt.

41st Division Administrative Instruction No.14 with
Amendment and Train Table is cancelled, and will be destroyed.
The attached is substituted.

                                                                Eric White
                                                                Major.
                                                                D.A.Q.M.G.
March 17th 1918.   41st Division.

Copies to:-

    122nd Infantry Brigade.
    123rd Infantry Brigade.
    124th Infantry Brigade.
    19th Middlesex.
    41st Divl.Signal Coy.
    "G".
    41st Divl.Train.
    A.D.M.S.
    D.A.D.V.S.
    D.A.D.O.S.
    A.P.M.
    C.R.E.
    Camp Commandant.
    D.M.G.O.
    C.R.A.
    File.
    War Diary.
    D.A.D.R.T.
    S.S.O.
    A.D.C. for G.O.C.
    Baths Officer.
    Gas Officer.
    238th Employment Coy.
    R.T.O. MONDICOURT.
    R.T.O. DOULLENS (North & South)
    Divl.Machine Gun Battalion.
    Divl. M.T.Company.

13th E. Surrey Regt

245/A/18

S E C R E T.

AMENDMENT TO 41st DIVISIONAL ADMINISTRATIVE INSTRUCTION
No.15 DATED 17th MARCH 1918.

20th March 1918.

In view of the move of the Division the following amendments are made to 41st Divisional Administrative Instruction No.15 dated 17th March 1918.

1. When the Division is in the BAIZIEUX Area –

   For MONDICOURT   road   EDGEHILL.

   " DOULLENS North. road   AVELUY.

   " DOULLENS South. road   ALBERT.

2. In the event of the Pioneer Battalion being detached from the Division at the time of the move the instructions contained in para.5 of the above quoted instruction will be carried out by each Infantry Brigade for its own entraining Station.
   Rations for the Platoons will be taken in all cases.

3. Should the move take place immediately after arrival in the BAIZIEUX area, surplus kits will be dumped and guarded in Brigade areas, under arrangements to be made by Brigades.

                                       Major,
                                   D. A. Q. M. G.,
                                   41st Division.

Copies to all recipients of 41st Divisional Administrative Instruction No.15 dated 17th March 1918.

41st DIVISION ADMINISTRATIVE INSTRUCTION No. 15.

17th March 1918.

1. With reference to 41st Division Order No. 224 of 9th March.

2. The Division will entrain in accordance with the attached table. Times of departure of the trains will be notified later.

3. ALL troops will report at Entraining Station <u>three</u> hours before the scheduled time of departure of the respective trains.

4. Each train will consist of the following vehicles :-

    30 Covered Trucks.
    17 Flat Trucks.
    1 Officers Coach.

5. The Officer Commanding the 19th Middlesex Regiment will detail one platoon to help load at each station. These platoons will report at their respective stations 3½ hours before the advertised time of departure of the first train. The Platoons will proceed on the last train from each station.
    Rations will be provided at the DOULLENS Stations, but must be taken by the platoons proceeding to MONDICOURT.

6. Units will entrain with the unexpired portion of the days rations plus rations for the day subsequent to entrainment on the man. The Officer Commanding Divisional Train will arrange on receipt of a warning wire from this office, to load supply vehicles from Supply Column in sufficient time for the Supply Wagons to entrain full.

7. Baggage and Supply Wagons will entrain with the units to which they are allotted.
    Baggage wagons will join units on receipt of warning wire.
    Supply wagons will join units as soon as they are loaded with the rations for the second day subsequent to entrainment (vide. para. 6.) or, in case of lack of time, will proceed direct to the entraining station.

8. <u>SURPLUS KIT.</u>
    In the event of a move at short notice all surplus kit should be sent forthwith to the D.A.D.C.S. Store.
    Officer in charge dumps will arrange to dump the Concert Party kit in this store and he will also leave behind sufficient personnel to receive and guard all surplus kits.
    No responsibility will be accepted for damage to or loss of kit deposited in this store.

9. ACKNOWLEDGE.

Major,
D. A. Q. M. G.,
41st Division.

A. & Q.

41st DIVISION.

APRIL 1918

Appendices attached

    Instructions.
    Casualty list
    Courts Martial Statement.

Army Form C. 2118.

WAR DIARY
or
INTELLIGENCE SUMMARY.

(Erase heading not required.)

"A" & "Q" 41st.Division.
April 1918.

Instructions regarding War Diaries and Intelligence Summaries are contained in F. S. Regs., Part II. and the Staff Manual respectively. Title pages will be prepared in manuscript.

Place	Date	Hour	Summary of Events and Information	Remarks and references to Appendices
St. AMAND.	3/4/18.		41st.Division less Artillery entrained at FREVENT and PETIT HOUVIN and moved to Second Army detraining at PROVEN and PESELHOEK.	(1).
STEEN-VOORDE.	4/4/18.		Divisional Headquarters established at STEENVOORDE.	
YPRES.	9/4/18.		Division moved into left sector VIIIth Corps front. - D.H.Q. at CANAL BANK YPRES.	(2).
VLAMER-TINGHE.	15/4/18.		Divisional Headquarters moved back to VLAMERTINGHE CHATEAU.	(3).
"	26th./4/18.		Administrative Instruction No.30 issued.	(4).
			A statement shewing Casualties in the Division for the month of April.	(5).
			A statement shewing Courts Martial for the month of April.	

Lieut.Colonel,
A.A.&.Q.M.G., 41st.Division.

APPENDIX 1

S E C R E T.

41st DIVISION ADMINISTRATIVE INSTRUCTION No.21.

1. The 41st Division (less Artillery) accompanied by Headquarters and three sections Mechanical Transport Company, will be transferred from Third Army to Second Army (8th Corps) by rail.

2. Entrainment will commence about 2.p.m. April 3rd 1918 at FREVENT and PETIT HOUVIN in accordance with attached table "A".

3. Entrainment will be directed by D.A.Q.M.G.

   Entraining Officers FREVENT :- Lieut Hogg,M.C.
   PETIT HOUVIN · Lt.Bennett.

   Detrainment will be directed by D.A.A.G.

   Detraining Officers. PROVEN :- Capt Quare,M.C.
   PRZELHOEK :- Capt Shone.

4. Personnel will report at Entraining Station one hour and Transport three hours before scheduled hour of departure of train.
   A.D.M.S. will arrange for an ambulance to be at each Entraining and Detraining Station.
   O.C.Signal Company will detail two despatch riders to report to Staff Officers in charge Entrainment and Detrainment.

5. Officer Commanding 19th Middlesex (Pioneers) will detail one Company to load trains at each of the Entraining Stations. These Companies will report to the R.T.O. 3½ hours before the time of departure of the first train from each station, and will proceed by the last train from each station respectively, namely train No.19 from FREVENT and train No.20 from PETIT HOUVIN.

6. The Officer Commanding each unit entraining will hand to the R.T.O. at entraining station, a state, in duplicate, showing the numbers of personnel, animals, (by classes) 4 wheeled and two wheeled vehicles to be entrained.

7. Supply and Baggage wagons will entrain loaded with units to which they are allotted.
   Baggage wagons will remain with units until completion of move.
   Supply wagons will join their units transport as soon as loaded with the rations with which they will entrain.

(2).

8. Transport of Brigades will march to Entraining Stations in Brigade Columns under Officer Commanding Train Company concerned, and Transport of Divisional Units under an Officer to be detailed by O.C.Train, to arrive at entraining station not less than three hours before scheduled hour of departure of train. In the case of units not entraining for some time after arrival in entrainment area, transport will join unit in their rest billets, and proceed to entraining station under orders of Commanding Officers concerned, also arriving not less than three hours before scheduled time of departure.
A.P.M. will detail sufficient police to accompany each column.

9. Busses will be provided by G.H.Q.Buss Park to convoy personnel from ~~HALLOY, P.B.~~ area to entraining stations on morning 3rd April in accordance with attached table "B". *THIEVRES*

10. DEBUSSING.
Units entraining at FREVENT will debuss on main DOULLENS - FREVENT road, between FREVENT and Farm LEROY.
Units entraining at PETIT HOUVIN will debuss on the main DOULLENS - ST POL Road between NUNCQ and PETIT HOUVIN.

11. At the embussing points units for PETIT HOUVIN must form up nearest the head of the column in each case, i.e. nearest to the destination.

12. The Senior Officer of each Group will, at the embussing point, arrange for the total party to be sub-divided into 20's and 25's* irrespective of overlapping of units, but keeping a break between the parties for different destinations.
(* A lorry holds 20 men. A bus holds 25 men.)
(For composition of bus columns see Table "B".)

13. Units will be in position on the embussing points 30 minutes before time of embussing vide Table "B".

14. A Staff Officer or representative will meet bus columns on arrival at debussing points and will indicate area where troops who are not entraining at once may rest until hour of entrainment.

15. The following will be the supply arrangements for the move :-

On 2nd April Divisional Train will deliver early rations for 3rd instant to units entraining in trains 1 to 11 (see Table "A"). Will refill rations for consumption 4th and join units.

On 3rd April Divisional Train will deliver rations for 4th instant to units entraining in trains 12 - 20 (see table "A") after their arrival in rest billets in entrainment area. Will refill in this area at Refilling Point to be arranged between O.C.Train and O.C.M.T.Company, and join units.

/on 4th

(3).

15. (continued). On the 4th April M.T. Company will dump rations for consumption 5th for units in trains 1 to 11 in Second Army Area and whole column refills first time in Second Army Area at WIPPENHOEK for consumption 6th instant.

16. The following additional transport has been asked for and will, subject to cancellation be as follows :-

  Divisional Headquarters 2 Lorries.
  Each Bde H.Q. 2 Lorries.

to report at respective Headquarters 7.a.m. 3rd instant and to convey baggage to Entraining Stations.

17. M.T. Company and Motor Ambulances will move by road on 3rd inst. under orders to be issued by O.C., M.T. Company and A.D.M.S.

  Route via DOULLENS - ST POL - LILLERS - AIRE - HAZEBROUCK, to STEENVOORDE.

18. ACKNOWLEDGE.

              [signature]
              Lieut Colonel,
              A.A. & Q.M.G.
April 1st 1918.   41st Division.

Distribution :-
  122nd Infantry Brigade. 123rd Infantry Brigade.
  124th Infantry Brigade. 19th Middlesex.
  Divl M.Gun Bn.   C.R.E.
  A.D.M.S.   Divisional Train.
  Mobile Vet. Section   Camp Commandant.
  Signal Company.   238 Employment Co.
  41st M.T. Company.   'G'.
  D.A.D.O.S.   D.A.D.V.S.
  A.P.M.   Capt Shone.
  Capt Quare.   Lt. Jarrett.
  Lt. Hogg.   R.T.O. FRUVENT
  R.T.O. PETIT HOUVIN. Second Army Q.
  VIII Corps Q.   4th Corps Q.
  S.A.A. Section D.A.C. 42rd Div Q.
  Transport Officers, 122, 123, 124, Brigade, 19th Msex and Divl M.Gun Bn.
  Posts.
  War Diary.
  File.

TABLE "B". EBUSSING PROGRAMME.

Detail.	Unit.	Point of Ebussing.	Entraining Station.	Time of Embussing.	Bus Column.
1.	Bde.H.Qrs and 8 Battalions 122 Brigade.	HARIEUX - THIEVRES road - head at THIEVRES facing North.	FREVENT.	9.a.m.	WILL BE NOTIFIED LATER
	228th.Field Coy. R.E.	- do -	PETIT HOUVIN.	9.a.m.	
	1 Company 19 Middlesex.	- do -	PETIT HOUVIN.	9.a.m	
	Bde.H.Qrs.and 3 Battalions 123 Brigade.	- do -	FREVENT.	9.a.m.	
	233 Field Coy. R.E.	- do -	PETIT HOUVIN.	9.a.m.	
2.	D.H.Q.,H.Q.Fs,41 Signal Coy.3rd Employment Coy.	PAS - LOTDICOURT road - head at LOTDICOURT facing North.	PETIT HOUVIN.	8.30.a.m.	
	Bde.H.Q.& 3 Bns 124th Brigade.	- do -	FREVENT.	8.30.a.m.	
	227th Field Co.	- do -	PETIT HOUVIN.	8.30.a.m.	
	Div M.Gun Br.	- do -	PETIT HOUVIN.	8.30.a.m.	
	138, 139, 140th F.Art.	- do -	PETIT HOUVIN.	8.30.a.m.	
	19th Middlesex. less 1 Coy.	- do -	FREVENT.	8.30.a.m.	

TABLE "A".

Entraining Stations A. FREVENT.
B. PETIT HOUVIN.

Train No. from Station. A. B.	UNITS.	Time and date of Departure.	Train No. from Station. A. B.	UNITS.	Time and Date of Departure.
1.	A.Rr.122 Bde & 122 F.H.Q.	3.20.p.m.3rd.	12.	No.4.Co.Div Train & 237 F.Co.	5.49.a.m.4th.
2.	½ SAA Sec. D.A.C.	2.49.p.m.3rd.	13.	A.Br.124 Bde & 124 F.H.Q.	9.20.a.m.4th.
3.	B Br.122 Bde & Bde Sig Sec.	6.20.p.m.3rd.	14.	138 Fld Amt & M.V.S.	9.49.a.m.4th.
4.	½ SAA Sec D.A.C.	5.49.p.m.3rd	15.	B.Br.124 Bde & Sig Sectr.	12.20.p.m.4th.
5.	C.Rr.122 Bde & T.M.B.	9.20.p.m.3rd.	16.	139 Fld Amt & H.Q.Div Train.	11.34.a.m.4th.
6.	No.2 Co.Train & 228 F.Co.	8.49.p.m.3rd.	17.	C.Br.124 Bde & T.M.B.	3.20.p.m.4th.
7.	A.Br.123 B. & 123 F.H.Q.	12.20.a.m.4th.	18.	Div M.Gun Bn.	2.49.p.m.4th.
8.	D.H.Q.,B.H.T.E., H.Q.& H.Q. Section Signal Co.	11.49.p.m.3rd.	19.	19th Msex less 1 Cooker, 4 G.S. Wagons & teams & 1 Company 140th Fld Amt plus 1 Company	6.20.p.m.4th.
9.	B.Br.123 Bde & Sig.Sectr. No.3 Co.Div Train, 233rd Field Co. & Emp. Company.	3.20.a.m.4th. 2.49.a.m.4th.	20.	1 Cooker, 4 G.S. Wagons & teams of 19th Middlesex.	5.49.p.m.4th.
10.					
11.	C.Br.123 Bde & T.M.B.	6.20.a.m.4th.			

SECRET.

APPENDIX 2

41st DIVISION ADMINISTRATIVE INSTRUCTION NO 25.
issued in connection with
41st Division Operation Order No. 239 dated 7/4/18.

1. **ACCOMMODATION.**
   On completion of relief the Division will be accommodated in Left Division Sector, VIIIth Corps Front, as shown in attached schedule.

2. **MOVES.**
   Headquarters Divisional Train, Mobile Vet Section will move to new area on 10th instant.

3. **SUPPLIES.**
   Supply Railhead for three Brigade Groups will be VLAMERTINGHE from 9th instant inclusive.
   Train will draw by Horse Transport refilling at Company Lines.
   As the M.T. Company is cut out, Divisional Train will hold one days rations in advance.
   Reserve rations are stored as follows and will be taken over by relieving units :-
   CALIFORNIA CAMP.   600 rations Pres.Meat & Biscuits.
   HALIFAX CAMP.   600   "   "   "   "   "
   M.Gun Bn.Camp.   300   "   "   "   "   "
   Rations for Right Sector go by limber to BELLEVUE.
   Rations for Left Sector go by limber to CORNERCOT.

4. **AMMUNITION.**
   Divisional Dump is at ST JEAN I.3.a.5.8.
   Right Bde Dump   WATERLOO   D.9.d.9.9.
                         KRONPRINZ   D.3.c.6.4.
   Right Brigade draw from ST JEAN by horse transport.
   Left Brigade draw from ST JEAN and load on to tramway trucks at BILGE DUMP C.28.d.8.3. for delivery by tram to KRONPRINZ.

5. **R.E.MATERIAL.**
   Divisional Dumps.   HOP FACTORY.   H.8.a.5.9.
                         BILGE   C.28.a.8.3.
                         SPREE FARM.   C.18.d.3.3.
                         ASSOUAN   D.8.c.0.0.
                         SEINE   D.16.d.3.5.
   Brigade Dumps.   WATERLOO   D.9.d.9.9.
                         KRONPRINZ   D.3.c.6.4.

/6.Provost.

APPENDIX 2.

6. PROVOST ARRANGEMENTS.
Will be taken over on 9th instant under arrangements to be made by A.P.Ms concerned.
In event of active operations Straggler Posts will be established :-
    No.1.   C.18.c.3.3.
    No.2.   C.24.a.1.7.
    No.3.   C.24.a.6.1.

7. MEDICAL ARRANGEMENTS.

    R.A.P's.   D.4.a.8.4.
               D.4.b.5.1.
               D.4.d.5.3.

    Relay Post.   D.10.c.5.9.

    A.D.S.   SOMME REDOUBT D.13.d.6.6.
              BRIDGE HOUSE   C.24.a.3.6.

    Corps M.D.S.   PRISON YPRES.

8. ORDNANCE.
Ordnance office and stores will be located at DIRTY BUCKET CAMP A.30.b.1.7.

9. VETERINARY.
Mobile Veterinary Section will be at G.5.b.7.6.

10. BATHS.
Divisional Baths will open on 9th instant at the following places :-
    (a). VLAMERTINGHE. capacity 80 men per hour.
    (b). DEAD END.   capacity 80 men per hour.

11. TRENCH FOOT CENTRE.
Divisional Trench Foot Centre will open on 9th instant at IRISH FARM CAMP C.26.d.8.7. capacity 800 per diem. Necessary ingredients for French System of Foot Treatment can be drawn from this hut, and used in camps where basins will be taken over.

3.

12. SALVAGE.
Divisional Salvage Dump is at C.27.c.9.5.
Salvage points are marked all along the main
WATERLOO - SPREE - WIELTJE - ST JEAN - YPRES Road.

13. DEFENCE SCHEME.
The Administrative arrangements 29th Divisional Defence Scheme will be taken over by Brigades on relief and will hold good till further orders.

14. ACKNOWLEDGE.

Lieut Colonel,
A.A. & Q.M.G.
41st Division.

April 7th 1918.

Copies to :- 122nd, 123rd, 124th Infantry Brigades.
C.R.E., 18th Middlesex, Divl M.Gun Bn.,
A.D.M.S., Divl Train, Divl Signal Co.,
S.S.O., A.P.M., D.A.D.O.S., D.A.D.V.S.,
"G", Baths, Salvage, Camp Commdt,
Employment Co., S.A.A.Sec.D.A.U.,
52rd M.V.S., 29th Divn Q., VIIIth Corps Q,
41st M.T.Co,. O.C.Crumps.

Location List to follow

LOCATION TABLE ISSUED IN CONTINUATION OF 41st DIVISION ADMINISTRATIVE INSTRUCTION No. 25 dated April 7th 1918.

Unit.	Personnel. Name of Camp.	Location.	Transport. Name of Camp.	Location.
Div H.Q.				
Adv.	Canal Bank.	I.1.b.7.8.	Mersey Lines	H.1.a.3.2.
Rear.	Mersey Farm.	H.1.a.1.3.	Mersey Lines	H.1.a.3.2.
Inf.Bde H.Q.				
Right Bde in Line.	Waterloo	D.9.d.8.9.		
Rear.	Eastbourne.	I.1.b.9.6.		
Left Bde in Line.	Kronprinz	D.3.c.7.5.		
Rear	Dead End.	I.1.b.9.6.		

Rear Brigade all at Road Camp all personnel and transport.
(St Tan 13c B:eyk:2)

Right Bde.				
1 Battln.			Nr.Reigersburg.	H.6.d.3.4.
2 Battlns & H.Q.			do	H.6.central
			Hagle.	G.5.d.central
Left Bde H.Q.				G.6.a.3.2.
1 Battln.			Hagle	G.5.d.central
1 Battaln.				A.29.d.6.3.
1 Battaln.				
M.G.Bn.				
H.Qrs.	Dead End.	I.2.c.2.6.	Ypres)	I.2.c.2.1.
3 Coys.	Line.		)	
1 Coy.	Support Camp	I.2.c.4.5.	)	
Details	Dead End Lock Camp.	I.1.b.7.0.	)	
				H.8.a.5.9.
C.R.E.	Canal Bank	I.1.b.7.8.		
1 Fld Co.	Line)	(Wieltje	(Warrington	H.2.c.1.4.
1 Fld Co.	Line)	(Dugouts &	(Camp	H.2.c.1.5.
	)	(St Jean	(	
	)	(Dugouts.		
1 Fld Co.	Webster Camp	H.3.c.6.4.	Moated Farm	H.2.d.8.2.

Pioneer Bn.	La Brique	C.26.d.5.1.	La Brique.	C.26.d.5.1.
M.Vet Sec.				G.5.b.3.6.
Ordnance.	Dirty Bucket Cp.	A.30.d.2.5.		
Employ Co.	Belgian Cp.	I.2.c.8.8.	Ypres	I.2.c.2.2.
M.M.P.	Ypres.	I.2.c.8.8.	HYDE CAMP AREA.	G.4.a.3.0.
Train Complete.				

Major
D.A.A.G. 41st.Divn.

April 7th 1918.

War Diary

41st.Divn.No.A.23/141.

PERSONNEL OF 29th.DIVISION WILL BE RELIEVED AS UNDER.

Date.	Offrs.	N.C.Os	Men.	Employment.	Location.	Remarks.	Found by.
April. 8th.		1	3	Baths.	VLAMERTINGHE.		Lt.Bonnett
		1	3	"	YPRES-DEAD END.		who will
		1	2	"	IRISH FARM.		live at DHQ.
		1	2	Trench Ft treatment.	Baths Dead End.	Fld.Amb.Pers.	A.D.M.S.
		1	2	Soup Kitch:	JALIFORNIA.	Extra to canteen pers.	A.D.M.S.
		1	2	" "	WIELTJE.	- do -	A.D.M.S.
April. 9th.		2	8	Camp Wardens.	St.JEAN.	Report Area Commandant.	124.Bde.
		2	23	Upkeep of dug-outs.	WIELTJE.	- do -	123.Bde.
		2	20	Loading R.E.Stores.	HOP FACTORY DUMP. H.8.a.5.9.	Report to R.E. at dump.	122.Bde.
		1	6	"	BILGE DUMP. C.28.a.8.1.	-do-	124.Bde.
		1	6	"	SPREE FARM. C.18.d.1.3.	-do-	124.Bde.
		1	4	"	MANNERS JUNCT:	-do-	124.Bde.
			2	Water Pt. Guard.	Depot Tank. I.7.a.5.5.		124.Bde.
	1	3	30	1/3 Burials. do (horses)	WIELTJE Dugouts. "	1 N.C.O.& 10 men from each Bde. 123.Bde. to supply officer	122.) 123.) 124.)
		1	50	Traffic Control.			A.P.M.
		1	4	Div.Bomb. Store.	St.JEAN DUMP.	S.A.A.,Sec. find Dump Offr.	124.Bde.
			2	Adv. do.	SPREE FARM.		123.Bde.
	1			Area Cmdt. St.JEAN.	I.3.a.9.9.		124.Bde.
	1			Area Cmdt. WIELTJE.	WIELTJE Dugouts. C.28.b.5.7.		123.Bde. 238th.
April. 10th.		1	3.	Gum Boots Store.	Store -Dead End.		Emp.Coy.

All Area Commandants are on the telephone.

[signature]
Major,
D.A.A.G., 41st.Division.

7/4/18.

Copies to:- 122nd.Infantry Brigade   A.D.M.S.
              123rd.   "   "   A.P.M.
              124th.   "   "   Baths Officer.
              S.A.A.Section.   "G".
              Divl.Employ;Coy.   29th.Division.
              C.R.E.   Spare.

SECRET.   APPENDIX 3

41st Division Administrative Instruction No.30.
reference 41st Division Order No. 245. dated 26/4/18.

1. MOVES.
    The following moves will take place forthwith.
    1st Line Transport 124th Inf.Bde to RYDE CAMP. G.4.c.3.9.
    41st M.G.Bn.Transport to Train Camps at G.4.d.5.7.& G.4.d.5.9.
    R.E.&.Pioneer Transport to BRAKE CAMP.G.6.a.9.9.
    41st Divl Train and Company 29th Divl Train to PEZELHOEK Camps

    "A" Echelons 1st Line Transport of Brigades, and any transport
    of other units which is required tactically may be ordered to
    positions as required by Brigadiers or Officers Commanding
    concerned.

2. TRANSPORT.
    Baggage wagons will report to units forthwith.

3. AMMUNITION.
    Divisional Dump will be at ORILLIA DUMP.H.2.c.2.7.
    The 124th Infantry Brigade will arrange tonight to move the
    123rd Infantry Brigade ammunition dump at ST JEAN and distribute
    as required along the YPRES defences, only leaving such
    ammunition in it as may be required by outpost line.

4. MEDICAL.
    Medical arrangements for YPRES defences will be :-
    Collecting Posts.   PRISON YPRES.
                         PILL BOXES. H.12.a.4.5.
    Car Post.   GOLDFISH CHATEAU.
    Advnced Dressing Stn.MOATED FARM.
    H.Q.Forward Fld Amb.RED FARM.
    Main Dressing Stn.   SCHOOL CAMP

5. R.E.MATERIAL.
    R.E.Dumps will remain as at present.

6. ACKNOWLEDGE.

                                        Lieut Colonel,
                                        A.A. & Q.M.G.
April 26th 1918.   41st Division.

Same distribution as 41st Divl Operation Order quoted above.
and TRANSPORT OFFICERS.

41st. DIVISION.

STATEMENT SHOWING CASUALTIES FOR MONTH OF APRIL 1918.

Unit.	OFFICERS.			OTHER RANKS.		
	Killed.	Wounded.	Missing.	Killed.	Wounded.	Missing.
41st.D.H.Q.	-	-	-	-	3	-
122nd.I.Bde.H.Qrs.	-	3	-	-	-	-
12th.E.Surrey R.	-	4	-	3	48	-
15th.Hants.R.	-	1	-	-	1	-
18th.K.R.R.C.	-	2	-	-	25	12
122nd.T.M.Bty.	-	-	-	-	-	-
123rd.I.Bde.H.Qrs.	-	-	-	-	-	-
11th.Queens.	-	-	-	1	32	14
10th.R.W.Kent R.	1	4	-	20	133	2
23rd.Middx.R.	-	1	1	5	14	8
123rd.T.M.Bty.	-	-	-	-	-	-
124th.I.Bde.H.Qrs.	-	-	-	-	-	-
10th.Queens.	-	2	-	6	23	2
26th.R.Fusrs.	-	3	-	4	28	1
20th.D.L.I.	-	-	2	3	29	18
124th.T.M.Bty.	-	-	-	-	-	-
19th.Middx. Regt.	-	2	-	3	56	-
41st.Div.M.G.Bn	-	3	-	11	55	-
41st.Divl.Arty.H.Q.	-	1	-	-	-	-
187th.Bde.R.F.A.	-	4	-	6	63	-
190th.Bde.R.F.A.	4	2	-	6	19	-
41st.D.A.C.	-	-	-	-	-	-
41st.Div.Signals.	-	-	-	-	25	-
H.Qrs.R.E.	-	-	-	-	-	-
228th.Field Coy.R.E.	1	-	-	-	1	-
233rd.Field Coy.R.E.	-	1	-	-	-	-
237th.Field Coy.R.E.	-	1	-	-	10	-
52nd.M.V.Sec.	-	-	-	-	-	-
138th.Fld.Amb.	-	6	-	1	35	-
139th. " "	-	-	-	-	4	-
140th. " "	-	-	-	-	7	-
41st.Div.Train.	-	1	-	1	6	-
238th.Emp.Coy.	-	-	-	2	4	-
Div.Gas Sch.	-	-	-	-	-	-
	6	41	3	73	616	57

APPENDIX 5

41st. DIVISION.
COURTS MARTIAL STATEMENT.
APRIL 1918.

Unit.	No. of Charges.	Charge.	Sentence.
15th. Hants. Regt.	4.	(2). Desertion.	Death. Commuted 10 Yrs. P.S.
		(1). Theft.	90 Days F.P.1.
		(1). Drunk.	Reduced to Cpl.
138th. Fld. Ambce.	1.	Absent without leave.	90 days F.P.1.
139th. Fld. Ambce.	1.	Drunkenness.	90 days F.P.1.
41st. Bn. M.G. Corps.	1.	Drunkenness.	Reduced to Sergeant.
19th. Middlesex.	1.	Striking Sup. Officer.	Not Guilty.
29th. Divl. Arty. D/17 Bty. R.A.	1.	Absent without leave.	Reduced to Cpl.
29th. D.A.C.	2.	(1). Sleeping at post.	90 days F.P.1.
		(1). Conduct to pred. of good order and Military Disc.	

CONFIDENTIAL.

WAR DIARY

OF

41st. DIVISION, "Q" BRANCH.

FROM May 1st. 1916.   TO, May 31st. 1916.

(VOLUME. 1.)

Army Form C. 2118

WAR DIARY
or
INTELLIGENCE SUMMARY
(Erase heading not required.)

Instructions regarding War Diaries and Intelligence Summaries are contained in F.S. Regs., Part II. and the Staff Manual respectively. Title Pages will be prepared in manuscript.

Place	Date	Hour	Summary of Events and Information	Remarks and references to Appendices
Aldershot	1-5-16		The Division commenced entraining, and via Southampton and Havre moved to France. F.	
Merris	4.5.16		The Division commenced to detrain at Godewaersvelde and Steenvoorde, and billeted about Outtersteene, Merris, Strazelle, Caestre, Pradelles, Borre and joined Second Army Second Corps.	
do	8.5.16		124th Infantry Brigade detrained at Steenbecque and billeted about Renescure, Ebblinghem, Staple and Wallon Cappel. Concentration of Division complete except D.A.C. which was kept at Havre. F.	
do	9.5.16		122 Infantry Brigade moved up and billeted about La Creche. 124 Infantry moved to Outtersteene and billeted about that place. F.	
do	9.5.16		Orders received for reorganisation of the division.	
do	do		Orders received for reorganisation of divisional mounted troops, divisional Royal Artillery & Corps Cavalry.	

Army Form C. 2118.

WAR DIARY
or
INTELLIGENCE SUMMARY.

41st. Division. "A" & "Q".

(Erase heading not required.)

May 1918.

Instructions regarding War Diaries and Intelligence Summaries are contained in F. S. Regs., Part II. and the Staff Manual respectively. Title pages will be prepared in manuscript.

Place	Date	Hour	Summary of Events and Information	Remarks and references to Appendices
La Lovie, BELGIUM.	May 9th.		Administrative Instruction No.31 issued.	Appendix.A
	May 31st.		Division under orders to be relieved in the YPRES Line and proceed by rail to Second Army training area. Divisional Headquarters moved from Vlamertinghe Chateau to Ten Elms Camp near Poperinghe on April 26th and from Ten Elms to La Lovie Chateau on April 29th remaining at La Lovie during the whole of May 1918.	
			Appendix "B" shows Courts Martial during the month of May.1918. Appendix "C" shows Casualties and Sick Evacuations during the month of May 1918.	Appendix.B Appendix.C

Major,
D.A.A.G.,
41st.Division.

27/6/18.

Army Form C. 2118.

WAR DIARY
or
INTELLIGENCE SUMMARY.

41st. Division. "A" & "Q".

May 1918.

(Erase heading not required.)

Instructions regarding War Diaries and Intelligence Summaries are contained in F. S. Regs., Part II. and the Staff Manual respectively. Title pages will be prepared in manuscript.

Place	Date	Hour	Summary of Events and Information	Remarks and references to Appendices
La Lovie, BELGIUM.	May 9th.		Administrative Instruction No.31 issued.	Appendix.A.
	May 31st.		Division under orders to be relieved in the YPRES Line and proceed by rail to Second Army training area. Divisional Headquarters moved from Vlamertinghe Chateau to Ten Elms Camp near Poperinghe on April 26th and from Ten Elms to La Lovie Chateau on April 29th remaining at La Lovie during the whole of May 1918. Appendix "B" shows Courts Martial during the month of May 1918. Appendix "C" shows Casualties and Sick Evacuations during the month of May 1918.	Appendix.B. Appendix.C.

27/6/18.

Major,
D.A.A.G.,
41st.Division.

Army Form C. 2118

WAR DIARY
or
INTELLIGENCE SUMMARY
(Erase heading not required.)

Instructions regarding War Diaries and Intelligence Summaries are contained in F. S. Regs., Part II. and the Staff Manual respectively. Title Pages will be prepared in manuscript.

Place	Date	Hour	Summary of Events and Information	Remarks and references to Appendices
STEENWERCK	30/5/16		The Divisional Headquarters moved to Steenwerck in relief of 9th Division leaving Yemmay and cyclists behind at Mouris. 9th Division Yeomany and cyclists left for training with Scouts Cavalry Division forming part of II Corps mounted troops	A B
do	31/5/16		Summary of Casualties for May are attached — Sick wastage —	

J.P. Hunt
Lt Colonel
A.A+Q.M.G.
A.A. Division

APPENDIX A

War Diary

SECRET.

41st DIVISION ADMINISTRATIVE INSTRUCTION NO.31.
Issued in connection with 41st Division Order
No.248 dated 9th May 1918.

1. AMMUNITION.

The 122nd Infantry Brigade will retain the same Ammunition Dump as at present.

The 124th Infantry Brigade will take over the Brigade Dump of the 16th Infantry Brigade at I.14.b.1.0. and report contents to Divisional Headquarters.

The Divisional Dump will remain at ORILLIA.

The 123rd Infantry Brigade will arrange to clear all Ammunition which may have been placed in Posts V.3 & V.4 to GOLDFISH DUMP.

All ammunition including S.O.S.Rockets in advance of Brigade Dumps in the Sectors affected will be handed over to 36th Division or taken over from 6th Division on relief.

2. SUPPLIES.

The 122nd Infantry Brigade will retain the 2,000 reserve rations held by them at each Battalion Headquarters E. of YPRES.

Authority has been asked for the issue of 1400 reserve rations to 124th Infantry Brigade for their two Battalions E. of YPRES.

Rations in the Sector to be taken over by the 124th Infantry Brigade Group nightly either to MENIN ROAD near ECOLE by N. of YPRES, or via KRUISTRAATHOEK & WARRINGTON Plank Road to just N.E. of SHRAPNEL CORNER. Northern route preferred.

Petrol Tins in the line will be handed over by 6th Division.

3. TRENCH STORES.

All Trench Stores, Sanitary arrangements, R.E.material, Gas Stores and Tools other than Mobilization Equipment will be left in situ.

4. MEDICAL ARRANGEMENTS.

RELAY POSTS. (i) The Prison, YPRES.
(ii) KRUISTRAAT I.13.c.2.9.
(iii) PILL BOXES H.12.a.8.8. H.12.b.2.8.

COLLECTING POSTS   ) (i) DEAD END, CANAL.
and ADVANCED   D.S.)   (ii) Farm at H.11.b.9.3. (Subsidiary)

A.D.S. & H.Q.   )
FORWARD FIELD AMBULANCE.) DIRTY BUCKET CAMP D.
    140th F.A.   )   A.30.central.

MAIN DRESSING STATION.   )
    138th F.A.   ) ROUSBRUGGE W.17.c.0.4. (Sheet 19)

SUBSIDIARY DRESSING STATION.) L'EBRE FARM F.29.d.5.9. (Sheet 27)
    139th F.A.   )

WALKING WOUNDED COLLECTING POST for Heavy Fighting) ORILLIA DUMP FARM

5. R.E. MATERIAL.

    Forward Dumps.   L.Sector ALABAMA Dump I.3.c.5.2.
                      R.Sector.SALLY PORT Dump I.8.d.0.3.
                      Posts V.3. V.4.KINCARDINE Siding H.5.8.7.7.

    Divl.Dump.   CULLODEN SIDING B.26.d.5.0.

6. There is practically no alteration in the Administrative Area of the Division West of the lines REIGERSBURG - THE ASYLUM & the existing Administrative arrangements hold good.

7. ACKNOWLEDGE.

(signature)

Lieut.Colonel.
A.A. & Q.M.G.
41st Division.

May 10th, 1918.

APPENDIX A

War Diary

S E C R E T.

41st DIVISION ADMINISTRATIVE INSTRUCTION NO.31.
Issued in connection with 41st Division Order
No.248 dated 9th May 1918.

1. **AMMUNITION.**

   The 122nd Infantry Brigade will retain the same Ammunition Dump as at present.

   The 124th Infantry Brigade will take over the Brigade Dump of the 16th Infantry Brigade at I.14.b.1.9. and report contents to Divisional Headquarters.

   The Divisional Dump will remain at CRILLIA.

   The 123rd Infantry Brigade will arrange to clear all Ammunition which may have been placed in Posts V.3 & V.4 to GOLDFISH DUMP.

   All ammunition including S.O.S.Rockets in advance of Brigade Dumps in the Sectors affected will be handed over to 36th Division or taken over from 6th Division on relief.

2. **SUPPLIES.**

   The 122nd Infantry Brigade will retain the 2,000 reserve rations held by them at each Battalion Headquarters E. of YPRES.

   Authority has been asked for the issue of 1400 reserve rations to 124th Infantry Brigade for their two Battalions E. of YPRES.

   Rations in the Sector to be taken over by the 124th Infantry Brigade Group nightly either to MENIN ROAD near ECOLE by N. of YPRES, or via KRUISTRAATHOEK & WARRINGTON Plank Road to just N.E. of SHRAPNEL CORNER. Northern route preferred.

   Petrol Tins in the line will be handed over by 6th Division.

3. **TRENCH STORES.**

   All Trench Stores, Sanitary arrangements, R.E.material, Gas Stores and Tools other than Mobilization Equipment will be left in situ.

4. **MEDICAL ARRANGEMENTS.**

   RELAY POSTS. (i) The Prison, YPRES.
   (ii) KRUISSTRAAT I.13.c.2.9.
   (iii) PILL BOXES H.12.a.8.8. H.12.b.2.8.

   COLLECTING POSTS   ) (i) DEAD END, CANAL.
   and ADVANCED   D.S.)   (ii) Farm at H.11.b.9.3. (Subsidiary)

   A.D.S. & H.Q.   )
   FORWARD FIELD AMBULANCE.) DIRTY BUCKET CAMP D.
   140th F.A.   )   A.30.central.

   MAIN DRESSING STATION.)
   138th F.A.   ) ROUSBRUGGE W.17.c.0.4. (Sheet 19)

   SUBSIDIARY DRESSING STATION.) L'EBRE FARM F.29.d.5.9. (Sheet 27)
   139th F.A.   )

   WALKING WOUNDED COLLECTING POST (For Heavy Fighting) CRILLIA DUMP FARM
   V.1.b.8.2.

(2)

R.E.MATERIAL.

 Forward Dumps. L.Sector ALABAMA Dump I.3.c.5.2.
         R.Sector.SALLY PORT Dump.I.8.d.0.3.
         Posts V.3. V.4.KINCARDINE Siding B.5.5.7.7.

 Divl.Dump.   CULLODEN SIDING B.26.d.5.0.

There is practically no alteration in the Administrative Area of the Division West of the lines REIGERSBURG - THE ASYLUM & the existing Administrative arrangements hold good.

ACKNOWLEDGE.

                 Lieut.Colonel.
                 A.A. & Q.M.G.
May 10th, 1918.   41st Division.

APPENDIX "B"

41st. DIVISION.

STATEMENT SHOWING COURTS MARTIAL FOR THE MONTH OF MAY 1918.

Unit.	No. of Cases.	Charge.	Sentence.
12th. E. Surreys.	1.	Absent without leave.	90 days F.P.1
15th. Hants Rgt.	1.	Disobeying an order.	90 days F.P.1.
18th. K.R.R.C.	3.	a. Desertion. b. Offence against property. c. Insub. language to Superior Officer.	10 yrs. P.S. Commuted to 3 yrs. Not Guilty. 60 days F.P.1.
23rd. Middx.	3.	a. Drunkenness. b. Conduct to Prejudice of Good order and Military Discipline. c. Sleep on Post.	42 days F.P.1. 56 days F.P.1. 5 years commuted to 60 days F.P.1
10th. R.W. Kent R.	1.	Neglect to prejudice of good order and Mil. Discipline.	28 days F.P.1
26th. R. Fusrs.	3.	(2). Conduct to prejudice of Good Order and Mil. Discipline. (1) Desertion.	(2). Not guilty. 10 yrs. P.S. 5 yrs remitted.
10th. Queens.	1.	Disobeying lawful command.	90 days F.P.1.
R.F.A.	1.	- do -	70 days F.P.1.
19th. Middlesex.	1.	Desertion.	10 yrs varied to 2 yrs. I.H.L.
233rd. Field Coy.	3.	(2). Desertion. (1). Drunkenness.	(1). 2yrs. I.H.L. (1). 1 yr. I.H.L. Reduced to ranks. Fined £1.

41st. DIVISION.

APPENDIX C

STATEMENT SHOWING CASUALTIES AND SICK WASTAGE FOR THE MONTH OF MAY 1918.

Unit.	Killed.	Wounded.	Missing.	Sick wastage.
12th. E. Surrey R.	1	3	-	22
15th. Hants. R.	-	5	-	31
18th. K.R.R.C.	-	1	-	35
11th. Queens.	-	6	1	51
10th. R.W. Kent R.	-	2	-	62
23rd. Middlesex.	-	5	-	60
10th. Queens.	-	3	-	26
26th. R. Fusrs.	-	2	-	56
20th. Durham L.I.	-	-	-	41
19th. Middlesex.	-	1	-	32
41st. Bn. M.G. Corps.	-	3	-	36
187th. Bde. R.F.A.	1	1	-	12
190th. Bde. R.F.A.	-	22	-	3
41st. D.A.C.	-	2	-	12
228th. Field Coy. RE.	-	1	-	7
237th. Field Coy. R.E.	-	5	1	4
233rd. Field Coy. R.E.	-	-	-	3
41st. Div. Train.	8	1	-	6
238th. Emp. Coy.	-	1	-	8
41st. Div. Sig. Coy.	-	-	-	5
138th. Field Amb.	-	-	-	4
139th. Field Amb.	-	-	-	9
140th. Field Amb.	-	-	-	8
41st. Div. M.T. Coy.	-	-	-	1
M.M.P.	-	-	-	1
	10	64	2	535

APPENDIX B

41st. DIVISION.

STATEMENT SHOWING COURTS MARTIAL FOR THE MONTH OF MAY 1918.

Unit.	No. of Cases.	Charge.	Sentence.
12th. E. Surreys.	1.	Absent without leave.	90 days F.P.1
15th. Hants Rgt.	1.	Disobeying an order.	90 days F.P.1.
18th. K.R.R.C.	3.	a. Desertion.	10 yrs. P.S. Commuted to 3 yrs.
		b. Offence against property.	Not Guilty.
		c. Insub. language to Superior Officer.	60 days F.P.1.
23rd. Middx.	3.	a. Drunkenness.	42 days F.P.1.
		b. Conduct to Prejudice of Good order and Military Discipline.	56 days F.P.1.
		c. Sleep on Post.	5 years commuted to 60 days F.P.1
10th. R.W.Kent R.	1.	Neglect to prejudice of good order and Mil. Discipline.	28 days F.P.1
26th. R. Fusrs.	3.	(2). Conduct to prejudice of Good Order and Mil. Discipline.	(2). Not guilty.
		(1) Desertion.	10 yrs. P.S. 5 yrs remitted.
10th. Queens.	1.	Disobeying lawful command.	90 days F.P.1.
R.F.A.	1.	- do -	70 days F.P.1.
19th. Middlesex.	1.	Desertion.	10 yrs varied to 2 yrs. I.H.L.
233rd. Field Coy.	3.	(2). Desertion.	(1). 2yrs. I.H.L. (1). 1 yr. I.H.L.
		(1). Drunkenness.	Reduced to ranks. Fined £1.

41st. DIVISION.

STATEMENT SHOWING CASUALTIES AND SICK WASTAGE FOR THE MONTH OF MAY 1918.

APPENDIX C

Unit.	Killed.	Wounded.	Missing.	Sick wastage.
12th.E.Surrey R.	1	3	-	22
15th.Hants.R.	-	5	-	31
18th.K.R.R.C.	-	1	-	35
11th.Queens.	-	6	1	51
10th.R.W.Kent R.	-	2	-	62
23rd.Middlesex.	-	5	-	60
10th.Queens.	-	3	-	26
26th.R.Fusrs.	-	2	-	56
20th.Durham L.I.	-	-	-	41
19th.Middlesex.	-	1	-	32
41st.Bn.M.G.Corps.	-	3	-	36
187th.Bde.R.F.A.	1	1	-	12
190th.Bde.R.F.A.	-	22	-	3
41st.D.A.C.	-	2	-	12
228th.Field Coy.RE.	-	1	-	7
237th.Field Coy.R.E.	-	5	1	4
233rd.Field Coy.R.E.	-	-	-	3
41st.Div.Train.	8	1	-	6
238th.Emp.Coy.	-	1	-	8
41st.Div.Sig.Coy.	-	-	-	5
138th.Field.Amb.	-	-	-	4
139th.Field.Amb.	-	-	-	9
140th.Field.Amb.	-	-	-	8
41st.Div.M.T.Coy.	-	-	-	1
M.M.P.	-	-	-	1
	10	64	2	535

41st DIVISION.

Daily Casualties. May 1916. Officers.

	14th.	19th.	24th
(1) 15th Bn. Hampshire Regt.	2 w.	1 s.w. at duty)	
(2) Field Companies, R.E.			1 w
(3) 189 Bruges RFA			

(1) Lieuts N Corbin and W Gregory
(2) Lieut R J Wacher
(3) Lieut R. J. Watts.

41st DIVISION.

DAILY CASUALTIES. MAY 1916. OTHER RANKS.

	10	11	12	13	14	15	16	17	18	19	20	21	22	23	24	25	26	27	28	29	30	31	Total.
122nd Bde.M.G.Coy.													2w*										2 w.
12th E.Surrey Regt.			1w																		1w*	2w	3 w.
15th Hampshire Regt.																					1w		9 w.
11th R.W.Kent Regt.			1w											1w							1w*	1w	5 w.
18th K.R.R.Corps.																					1k)		1 k. 2 w.
10th R.W.Kent Regt.									1w.												1w)		1 k. 1 w.
20th Durham L.Infy.																					7w. 1k.	1w.	1 k. 8 w.
10th R.W.Surrey Regt.						2w.													2w*				2 w.
32nd Royal Fusiliers.																			2w*				4 w.
21st K.R.R.Corps.																			1w*				1 w.
19th Middlesex Regt.	1w*			1w					1w						5w								11 w.
228th Field Coy.R.E.															1w								1 w.
233rd Field Coy.R.E.											1w					3w			2w				5 w.
128th Field Amb'ce.																					1w#		1 w.

Total.   2 k. 51 w.

Wounded include 10 accidental.
* Accidental.
# M.T.,A.S.C. attached.

41st DIVISION.

DAILY SICK WASTAGE.   MAY 1916.   OTHER RANKS.

UNIT.	8	9	10	11	12	13	14	15	16	17	18	19	20	21	22	23	24	25	26	27	28	29	30	31	Total
122 Bde. M.G.Coy.																								1	1
12th E.Surrey Rgt.		3	3	1	1	1	1			1			1	1	1	1	1	1	1					1	19
15th Hants. Regt.			1	3		1	3	1	1	1	1		1	3	1	1	6	1*	1	1	2		2	1	19
11th R.W.Kents.				2	1	1					1	4	1		1			1	3				1		12
18th K.R.R.Corps.							2		1			2	1						2						4
11th R.W.Surreys.	1	1	1			1	1	2	1	1	1		1	3	1	2		1		1	1	1			15
10th R.W.Kents.			3	3	1	3		1					1	1	2		1					2			10
23rd Middlesex.			1				1				1			1	1	1	1	1	1	1	1				7
20th Durham L.I.					1			2		1				2	1	1		3		1		1	2		11
10th R.W.Surreys.			1		3	3	1	1	1		1		1	1	2	2	1	1	1	1	1				14
26th R.Fusiliers.				1						1				2		1					1				9
32nd R.Fusiliers.					2		2					2	1	1	2	2	1		1		1		1		:20
21st K.R.R.Corps.	2	4							1	1	1	1	1	1			1	1	1		1				8
19th Middlesex.																									5
41st Div.Cyclist Co.	2	2	2		2												1								7
187th Bde. R.F.A.		1								1					2		2								7
189th Bde. R.F.A.				1			1										1					2	1		9
190th Bde. R.F.A.	1										1	1	1	1		1	1	1		1	1				4
183rd Bde. R.F.A.			1		6	1	1	1	1		1	1	1	1											1
41st Div.Amm.Col.																									1
233rd Field Coy.R.E.																									2
41st Div.Signal Co.														1											16
41st Divl. Train.			1	1	1	1	1	1	1	1	1	1	1	1			1				1		1		4
138th Field Amb'ce.																	1						1		:2
139th Field Amb'ce.																									5
140th Field Amb'ce.																							1	1	1
"B" Sq.1/1 Wilts.Yeo																									

Total wastage.   218.

C O N F I D E N T I A L

War Diary
of
A.A. & Q.M.G.,
41st. Division.

From 1/6/16 to 30/6/16.   (Volume 2).

WAR DIARY
or
INTELLIGENCE SUMMARY.

'A' and 'Q' 41st. Division.
June 1918.

(Erase heading not required.)

Army Form C. 2118

Place	Date	Hour	Summary of Events and Information	Remarks and references to Appendices
Lovie Chateau.	June 3rd.		Division commenced to move to Second Army Training Area. Divisional Headquarters moved to Nieulet.	A & B.
Nieulet.	June 9th.		Divisional Headquarters moved to EPERLECQUES.	'C'.
EPERLECQUES.	June 24th.		Orders issued for move to Second Army front to relieve 7th French Division.	
	June 27th.		Divisional Headquarters moved to OUDERZEELE.	'D'.
	"	"	Instructions for relief issued.	E
	June 30.		Divisional Headquarters moved to La Linge.	F
			A statement shwoing Courts Martial is attached.	
			A statement shewing casualties is attached.	

Major,
D.A.A.G.,
41st.Division.

Army Form C. 2118

WAR DIARY
or
INTELLIGENCE SUMMARY
(Erase heading not required.)

17

Place	Date	Hour	Summary of Events and Information	Remarks and references to Appendices
STEENWERCK			No movements of importance took place during the month of June. Attached are tables showing (1) Nominal roll of officers killed, wounded and missing during the month (2) Numbers of other ranks killed, wounded and evacuated sick during the month (3) Statement showing numbers washed in divisional baths during the month J B Knox Lt Col. AA & QMG 10/7/16 41st Divn	

APPENDIX "A"

SECRET.

41st Division Administrative Instruction No.32

reference 41st Division Operation Order No. 252

dated 1st June 1918.

1. The attached schedule shows the Light Railway Programme for withdrawal of troops of the Division to the ST JAN TER BIEZEN area.

2. The Division will, after withdrawal, entrain in tactical trains in accordance with a time table and instructions to be issued later for conveyance to Second Army Training Area.

3. Brigades and other troops of the Division who spend a night in the Staging area will be accommodated there as follows :-

123rd Infantry Brigade.	SCHOOL CAMP L.2.d.
2 Battalions.	M. and N Camps.
122nd Infantry Brigade.	ROAD CAMP.L.2.a.2.8.
19th Middlesex Rgt.	L.4.b.2.5. near St JAN ter BIEZEN.
Machine Gun Bn.	F.27.a.2.6. " " "
3 Field Companies.	L.3.b.7.8.
	L.3.b.7.9.
	L.3.b.3.7.
2 Field Ambulances.	L.3.a.8.4. and F.25.d.7.8.

Transport of units relieving on nights 2nd/3rd will march on evening 2nd to Staging Area.

4. Divisional Train (less No.1 Company) and 1st Line Transport of units (less those vehicles entraining in tactical trains, to be specified later) S.A.A.Section D.A.C. and Mobile Veterinary Section will march on 3rd instant in accordance with attached March Table staging for night 3rd/4th in ZEGGERS CAPEL area (billets on application to Area Commandant there), rejoining their units in the Second Army Training Area on the 4th instant.

5. The Divisional Train (less No.1 Company) will dump rations, less those of 1st Line Transport, for consumption 4th before marching 3rd as follows, leaving sufficient personnel to issue to units :-

122nd Inf.Bde.	ROAD CAMP.
123rd Inf.Bde.	SCHOOL CAMP.
124th Inf Bde.	PUGWASH Station.
M.Gun Bn.	F.27.a.26. Nr.St JAN Ter BIEZEN.
19th Middlesex.	L.4.b.2.5. " " "
3 Fld Co R.E.	SCHOOL CAMP L.3.b.7.8.
138 & 140 Fld Amb.	ROUSBRUGGE (138 F.A.H.Q.)
139 Fld Amb.	L'EBBE Farm.
D.H.Q.& Emp Co.	LOVIE CHATEAU.

Guides from 122nd Bde units will meet their supply wagons at entrance to ROAD CAMP at 8.a.m. 3rd June and guides from 123 Brigade units at road junction L.4.b.8.2.

(ii).

Units will arrange for party to take over the above rations from Divisional Train by 10.a.m. 3rd instant.

The Train will march empty, refilling on evening of 3rd in ZEGGERS CAPEL area with supplies for consumption 5th.

Refilling Points to be fixed between O.C.Train and O.C.41st M.T.Company.

Supplies for consumption 5th will be delivered to units on arrival in Second Army Training Area.

Preserved Meat will be issued as far as possible for consumption 4th instant.

6. Accommodation of Division in Second Army Training Area will be issued later.

7. Baggage wagons will report to units on 2nd instant

One lorry per Brigade and one G.S.wagon per Light Trench Mortar Battery will be at disposal of Brigades for move from Line to Entraining Station. Brigades will notify times and place required.

8. All ammunition, reserve rations, petrol tins, solidified alcohol, gum boots, gas clothing, and other trench stores, will be handed over to 49th Division on relief, and a copy of receipt forwarded to Divisional Headquarters.

9. Relief of Traffic Control personnel will take place under arrangements to be made between A.P.Ms concerned.

10. The men of the Salvage Section now with Infantry Brigades in the Line will be returned to the Salvage Section by 12 noon 2nd instant. The Salvage Section will be relieved by 12 noon 3rd instant by 49th Division and will return to Divisional Headquarters that afternoon.

11. The S.A.A.Section and Divisional Ammunition Dump personnel will be relieved by 12 noon 3rd instant.

12. Brigades will detail an Officer to superintend the Light Railway entraining and arrange for guides to meet parties coming from the Line, and conduct to entraining siding.

Similar arrangements will be made at Light Railway detraining stations.

13. All camps and billets will be handed over in a thoroughly sanitary and clean condition.

14. Divisional Baths will close on the morning of the 2nd instant.
Divisional Canteen on the morning of the 3rd instant.

15. ACKNOWLEDGE.

Lieut Colonel,
A.A. & Q.M.G.
41st Division.

June 1st 1918.

Copies to :-
122nd Brigade.	123rd Brigade.	124th Brigade.
C.R.A.	C.R.E.	19th Middlesex.
M.G.Bn.	Camp Commdt.	Employment Co.
Signal Co.	Mob Vet Secn.	D.A.D.O.S.
D.A.D.V.S.	"G"	A.P.M.
Divl Train.	41 M.T.Company.	S.S.O.
49th Division.	IInd Corps. Q.	Baths.
Canteen.	A.D.M.S.	File

TABLE OF LIGHT RAILWAY TRAINS.

Date.	Unit.	Entraining Station.	Detraining Stn.	No.of men 300 each.	No.of trains	Remarks.
night 2nd/3rd.	1st I.Bde.	FORWARD DUMP.	RUBY SIDING.	2000.	7.	To wait after bringing up troops of 40 Division to pick up units of 41 Divn when relieved.
"	2 Coys Pioneers.	- do -	- do -	450	2	"
"	1 Coy M.G.Bn.		- do -	150		"
"	H.Q.& 1 Coy Pioneers.	CULLODEN SIDING.	- do -	300	1	In position 6.p.m.
3rd instant.	124th I.Bde.	MISSION SIDING.	PUGWASH.	600	2	To wait after bringing troops of 40th up. Should be ready to start loading 10.15.a.m.
"	"	ORILLIA or MAHIM.	- do -	900	3	"
"	"	EAGLE.	- do -	900	3	"
"	1 Co.M.G.Bn.	EAGLE	- do -	150	1	"
"	1 Co.M.G.Bn. 233rd Fld Co.	EAGLE	RENN SIDING	500	1	To wait at EAGLE after taking up troops of 40 Divn. to pick up units of 41 Divn when relieved.
night 3rd/4th.	122nd I.Bde.	MACHINE GUN SIDING	PUGWASH	2000	7	To wait after taking up troops of 40 Divn to pick up units of 41 Divn when relieved.
"	1 Coy M.G.Bn.	MACHINE GUN SIDING	RUBY SIDING	150	1	"

MARCH TABLE OF TRANSPORT.

Date.	Serial No.	Unit.	From.	To.	Starting Point.	Time.	Route.
3rd.June.	1.	No.2.Coy.Div.Train. 1st.Line Tpt.122.I.B. (less that proceeding by train). 228th.Field Coy.R.E.	IInd Corps. Area.	ZEGGERSCAPPEL.	X Roads. F.21.a.2.6.	9.a.m.	Via HOUTKERQUE – WOREHOUDT.
3rd.June.	2.	No.3 Coy.Div.Train. 1st.Line Tpt.123.I.B. " " 233rd. Field Coy.R.E. 1st.LineTpt.139th. Field Ambulance.	-do-	-do-	-do-	9.45 a.m.	- do -
3rd.June.	3.	No.4 Coy.Div.Train. 1st.Line Tpt.124.I.B. " " 235th. Field Coy.R.E. 1st.Line Tpt.140th. Field Ambulance.	-do-	-do-	-do-	10.30 a.m.	- do -
3rd.June.	4.	H.Q.Div.Train. Divl.H.Qrs. 19th.Middlesex. S.A.A. Sec. D.A.C. M.G.En. Div.signal Coy. Mob.Vet.Section.	-do-	-do-	-do-	11.15 a.m.	- do -
4th.June.	1.	No.2 Coy. Div.Train. 1st.Line.Tpt.122.I.B. (less that proceeding by train) 228th.Field Coy.R.E.	ZEGGERS- CAPPEL.	IInd Army Training Area.	ERKELSBRUGGE. X Roads.	8.0 a.m.	Not yet known Definitely.

/OVER.

MARCH TABLE OF TRANSPORT. (cont'd)

Date.	Serial No.	Unit.	From.	To.	Starting Point.	Time.	Route.
4th June.	2.	No.3 Coy.Divl.Train. 1st Line Transport 123.I.B. " " 233rd Field Coy.R.E. 1st Line Tpt.159th Field Ambulance.	ZEGGERSCAPPEL.	II Army Training Area.	ERKELSBRUGGE X Roads.	8.45 a.m.	Not yet known definitely.
4th June.	3.	No.4.Coy.Div.Train. 1st Line Tpt.124.I.B. " " 237th. Field Coy.R.E. 1st Line Tpt.140th Field Ambulance.	-do-	-do-	-do-	9.30 a.m.	-do-
4th June.	4.	H.Q.Div.train. Divl.H.Qrs. 19th Middlesex. S.A.A.Sec.,D.A.C. M.G.Battalion. Divl.Signal Coy. Motile Vet.Sec.	-do-	-do-	-do-	10.15 a.m.	-do-
4th June.	5.	138th Field Amb.co.	ROUSBRUGGE.	ZEGGERSCAPPEL.	ROUSBRUGGE.	7.0. a.m.	Via HERZEELE-WORMHOUDT.
5th June.	5.	138th Field Amb.co.	ZEGGERSCAPPEL.	II Army Training Area.	ZEGGERSCAPPEL.	7.0. a.m.	Not yet known.

Note:- 1. The O.C. Train Company will be in command of each Brigade Group Transport.
O.C. Train will be in Command of Divl.H.Q. Group Transport.
2. Gaps of 50 yards will be maintained between each 6 vehicles, and 150 yards between transport of each Unit.
3. The A.P.M. will arrange Police for necessary control.

APPENDIX "B"

SECRET.

Further Administrative Instructions in
continuation of 41st Division Administrative Instruction
No. 32 dated June 1st 1918.

1. The Division will move to Second Army Training Area by tactical trains in accordance with attached schedule "A".

2. No baggage may be taken in the personnel trains, with the exception of a limited number of cooking utensils in the case of the first and second groups.

3. Transport will be at the station three hours, and personnel one hour before scheduled time of departure of train.

4. Entrainment will be supervised by D.A.Q.M.G.
   Detrainment by D.A.A.G.

5. Loading and unloading parties of 3 Officers and 100 men will be found from the R.E.Companies travelling by transport trains 4 and 7.
   They will report to Staff Officer for entrainment three hours before scheduled hour of departure of these trains.

6. Schedule "B" shows the transport of 122nd and 123rd Infantry Brigades and Machine Gun Battalion which will proceed by rail (this cancels instructions issued with March Table as far as it concerns 123rd Infantry Brigade First Line Transport and Machine Gun Bn 1st Line Transport).

7. Schedule "C" shows the accommodation allotted to units in Second Army Training Area.
   The position of Divisional Headquarters will be notified later.

8. Billeting parties should be sent on by road early on 3rd instant to arrange billets with Area Commandants concerned.

9. Supply Railhead, except for Artillery, will be WATTEN from 5th June inclusive.

10. ACKNOWLEDGE.

June 2nd 1918.

Lieut Colonel,
A.A. & Q.M.G.
41st Division.

Issued to all recipients of 41st Divl Administrative Instn
No.32.

SCHEDULE "A".

Serial No.	Date.	Class of Train.	Units.	Entraining Station.	Detraining Station.	Time of Departure.	Time due to arrive.	REMARKS.
1	June 3rd.	Persnnl.	124 I.Fde. (less weakest Bn.a.T.M.B.) .G.In.1 Company.	PROVEN	WATTEN	15.00	18.30.	
2	3rd.	Transport used as personnl.	1 Bn.124 I.Fde. (weakest). 124 T.M.B. 1 Fld Amb. 1 Fld Co.R.E.	PROVEN	WATTEN	16.00.	19.30.	This train contains 1r flats on which baggage may be loaded, but must be unloaded and dumped immediately on arrival.
3	June 4th	personnl.	123rd I.Fde less T.M.B.	PROVEN	WATTEN	03.00	06.30.	
4	4th	transport	123 I.M.B. 1 Fld C.R.E. transport as per schedule "B". 1 Coy M.g.Bn.	PROVEN	ST OMER	08.00	11.30	A limited amount of baggage can be loaded on spare flats or under loaded vehicles. Baggage must to unloaded and dumped immediately on arrival.
5.	4th	Persnnl.	H.Q., Employ Co 19th .sex, H.Q.Bn H.Q. and 1 Company. 1 Fld Ambnce. HQ Signal Co.	PROVEN	WATTEN	12.00	15.30.	
6.	4th	Personnl	122nd I.Fde less T.M.B.	PROVEN	WATTEN	20.00	23.30.	

Serial No.	Date.	Class of Train.	Units.	Entraining Station.	Detraining Station.	Time of Departure.	Time due to arrive.	REMARKS.
7	June 4/5th	Transport	1 Field Co.R.E. 1 Fld Ambince. M.G.M.1 Company 122 T.M.B. Transport as per schedule "B".	PROVEN	ST OMER	22.00	02.00	A limited amount of baggage can be loaded on spare flats or under loaded vehicles.

Composition of "Personnel" Train.

    1 Coach.
    4? Covered Trucks. (40 men per truck).

Composition of "Transport" Train.

    1 Coach.
    50 Covered Trucks.
    15 Flats.

=*=*=*=*=*=*=*=*=*=*=*=*=*=*=*=*=*=

41st DIVISION.

SCHEDULE "B".

Showing Transport and Personnel to travel on each Transport Train.

	Personnel.	Axles.	Horses.
Bde.H.Qtrs & 1 L.G.S.Wagon and team.	20	2	9.
Signal Section.	28	2	9.
From each Battalion (4 G.S.L.Wagons.	12	24	24
" " " (1 Water Cart.	3	3	6
" " " (1 Mess Cart.	3	3	3
" " " (2 Travelling Kitchens.	6	12	12
" " " (1 Maltese Cart.	3	3	3
" " " (11 Riding Horses and 6 Pack.	51		51
Machine Gun Battalion. 6 G.S.Lim Wagons.	9	12	18
" " " 2 Riding Horses.	2		2

"6"

Billeting schedule in connection with 41st Division
Administrative Instruction No.32 dated 1/6/18.

Billeting accommodation in New Area. (Hazebrouck 5A.)

122nd Brigade H.Qtrs.	GANSPETTE.
1 Battalion.	RAVENGHEM.
1 Battalion.	OUEST MONT & EST MONT.
1 Battalion.	HELLEBROUCQ.
R.e., Fld Amb.& R.M.B.	LE COMMUNAL.
Train Company.	BLUE MAISON.
Baths.	EPERLECQUES (39th Divn).

All details of billets from Area Commdt EPERLECQUES.

123rd Brigade Headquarters.	ST MOMELIN.
Fld Amb & T.M.B.	ST MOMELIN.
1 Battalion.	ROONEGHEM.
1 Battalion.	HALTE & NIEURLET (E) (HAVERSHERGUE FARM Bn. H.Q.)
1 Battalion.	MAISON ROUGE, Fme du HAM and LOTENBROUCK, farm (near LA PANNEL)(plus 20 tents)
R.E. and Train Co.	KINDERBELCK.
Baths.	ST MOMELIN.
Bathing.	Several good places on canal.

All details of billets from Area Commdt ST MOMELIN.

124th Brigade Headquarters.	WULVERDINGHE.
1 Battalion.	WULVERDINGHE.
1 Battalion.	CROME STRAETE.
1 Battalion.	LEDERZEELE Station. & South.
T.M.B and R.E.	BROXEELE South.
Fld Ambulance.	Les 5 Rues.
Train Company.	just East of CROME ST.
Baths.	WULVERDINGHE.
19th Middlesex.	RUYSSCHEURE.
M.Gun Battalion.	RUYSSCHEURE.
D.A.C.	RUYSSCHEURE.

All details of billets from Area Commdt LEDERZEELE.

Copies to all concerned and Area Commandants.

Major,
D.A.A.G.
41st Division.

2/6/18.

APPENDIX C

SECRET.

41st DIVISION ADMINISTRATIVE INSTRUCTION No.34
issued in connection with 41st Division Order No.256
dated 25/6/18.

1. Billeting parties of Infantry Brigade Groups and Divisional Troops less 41st Divisional Artillery will report to Staff Officer 41st Division at ARNEKE Church 7.30.a.m. tomorrow.
Billeting parties for 41st Divisional Artillery should report to British Liaison Officer with Artillery Headquarters 14th French Corps at WALMU.

2. Supplies for consumption 27th will be drawn from Railhead by 41st Divisional M.T.Company and delivered to Divisional Train Companies on arrival in new area at Refilling points to be arranged between O.C.Train and O.C.Divl M.T.Company. O.C.Train will notify time and place of refilling to units, who will send guides to refilling points.

3. One additional lorry for reconnoitering parties 122nd Infantry Brigade will report RUBROUCK Church 8.a.m. to proceed to vicinity of ABEELE.

4. Transport of Divisional Headquarters, R.E.Headquarters, and Headquarters Divisional Train will march to OUDEZEELE tomorrow via BALEMBERG and WEMAERS CAPPEL, not to leave LEDERZEELE till 124th Infantry Brigade Group is clear of that point.

5. Mobile Veterinary Section will remain with D.A.C. and march under orders of C.R.A.

6. A.P.M. will arrange for control of traffic during the march.

7. A.D.M.S. will make necessary arrangements for the collection of sick from columns unaccompanied by Field Ambulance.

ACKNOWLEDGE.

Lieut Colonel,
A.A. & Q.M.G.
41st Division.

June 25th 1918.

Destribution :-

122nd Inf.Brigade.	123rd Infantry Brigade.
124th Infantry Brigade.	C.R.A.
C.R.E.	A.D.M.S.
19th Middlesex.	Machine Gun Bn.
Divisional Train.	Signal Company.
238th Employ Co.	Mobile Vet Section.
D.A.D.O.S.	D.A.D.V.S.
A.P.M.	Camp Commandant.
"G".	Reception Camp.
Gas Officer.	Baths Officer.
41st M.T.Company.	39th Division.
S.S.O.	VIIth Corps "Q".

S E C R E T.

41st DIVISION ADMINISTRATIVE INSTRUCTION No.33

issued in connection with 41st Division Order No.255
dated 24/6/18.

1. Billeting parties should report for billets to Area Commandants' as follows:-

   R.A.   ZEGGERS CAPPEL.
   122nd Inf.Bde.Group.   RUBROUCK.
   123rd Inf.Bde.Group.   ST.MOMELIN.
   124th Inf.Bde.Group.   LEDERZEELE.
   Pioneers &)
   M.G.Battn.)   LEDERZEELE.

2. Supplies for consumption 26th will be drawn from Railhead on the 25th as on 24th and delivered to Units on arrival.

   On 26th instant Divisional M.T.Company will draw for all Units at Railhead and deliver to Refilling Points as arranged between them and O.C. Divisional Train.

3. Baggage wagons will be sent to Units forthwith.

   Extra transport will be allotted as follows and will report 8 a.m. 25th instant :-

   Royal Artillery.   4 Lorries to 187th Bde.H.Q.
   122nd Brigade.   5 Lorries to Bde.H.Q.
   123rd Brigade.   5 Lorries (one to each of the Bn.H.Q.
                                  and 2 to Bde H.Q.)
   124th Brigade.   5 Lorries (one to each of the Bn.H.Q.
                                  and 2 to Bde H.Q.)
   M.G.Battn.   1 Lorry to Bn.Headquarters.
   19th Middlesex.   1 Lorry to Bn.Headquarters.

   These lorries can remain with units until the night of the 26th when they will be returned to Divl.M.T.Company. Lorries should try and use different routes to marching troops.

4. A.D.M.S. will make necessary arrangements with G.Os.C. Brigades and O.C.Pioneer and Machine Gun Battalions for ambulances to follow the columns.

5. Mobile Veterinary Section will be attached to the D.A.C. during the move and will march tomorrow under orders from G.O.C. R.A.

6. A.P.M. will make necessary arrangements for traffic control during the march.

7. Divisional Headquarters, H.Q.R.E., and H.Q.Divisional Train will move under separate arrangements to be notified later.

8. Divisional Baths and Canteen will close tomorrow.

   Baths will return all dirty clothing to laundry, any clean clothing to be collected to EPERLECQUES Baths for transportation to new area.

9. Standing Orders of Second Army Training Areas will be complied with.

Amount of ammunition handed over to Sub-Area Commandants' will be notified to this office.

10. All billets will be left in a clean and sanitary condition and a certificate to this effect rendered to Sub-Area Commandants' concerned.

Rear parties should be left for a few hours to ensure that those orders are carried out.

11. The Divisional Reception Camp will remain in their present billets till further orders.

The water cart from the 124th Infantry Brigade and G.S.L. wagon from 123rd Infantry Brigade will be returned forthwith to their units.

Remaining transport lent to Divisional Reception Camp will be retained by them for the present.

Supplies for consumption 26th instant will be delivered direct to Camp by Divisional M.T.Company.

For the purpose of drawing supplies for consumption on 26th and after the 39th Division are sending 2 G.S.wagons to report to R.S.O.LUMBRES. These wagons will draw supplies daily commencing 26th instant at LUMBRES Railhead, and deliver to the Divisional Reception Camp.

ACKNOWLEDGE.

Lieut Colonel,
A.A. & Q.M.G.
41st Division.

June 24th 1918.

Copies to :-
```
122nd Infantry Brigade.        123rd Infantry Brigade.
124th Infantry Brigade.        C.R.A.
C.R.E.                         A.D.M.S.
19th Middlesex                 41st M.Gun Bn.
Divisional Train.              Signal Company.
238th Employ Co.               52nd Mob Vet Section.
D.A.D.O.S.                     D.A.D.V.S.
A.P.M.                         Camp Commandant.
"G".                           Divl Reception Camp.
Divl Gas Officer.              Baths Officer.
41st Divl M.T.Company.         O.C.Canteen.
VIIth Corps "Q".               39th Division "Q".
S.S.O.
```

Addition to 41st Divl Administrative Order No.33
dated 24/6/18.

Add para 14 as follows :-

14. Sick who are being treated regimentally and who
are unfit to march will be evacuated to the affiliated
Field Ambulance forthwith.
Artillery sick to 138th Fld Ambulance.

W. Cumming Miller
Lieut Colonel,
A.A. & Q.M.G.
41st Division.

June 24th 1918.

War Diary APPENDIX "D"

SECRET.

41st DIVISION ADMINISTRATIVE INSTRUCTION No.35
issued in connection with 41st Division Order
No.257 dated 27th June 1918.

1. ACCOMMODATION.

   (a). On completion of relief the Division will be accommodated in accordance with the attached table "A".

   (b). First Line Transport of units will take over the sites now occupied by corresponding units of the 7th French Division on relief, where transport in the case of Battalions is disposed in two echelons.

   (c). The Divisional Train will be accommodated in the area north of STEENVOORDE.

   (d). R.A.Wagon Lines and D.A.C. will remain in their present positions until relief is complete, when re-adjustment will be made.

   (e). Any re-adjustment of the accommodation in the area will be carried out after relief is complete.

2. AMMUNITION.

   (a). Artillery Ammunition.
   Arrangements are being made by C.R.A. to dump 300 rds per 18 pdr and 300 rds per 4.5" How in Battery positions previous to relief, to be increased to 400 rds as soon as possible.
   Indents for Artillery ammunition will be wired to Divisional Headquarters, who, on receipt of authority from Army, will arrange to draw and deliver to D.A.C.

   (b). S.A.A. and Grenades etc.
   Table "B" attached shows establishment allotted as Battalion, Brigade, and Divisional Reserve.
   Divisional Dump will be situated at L.34.a.9.7. and can be drawn on by Brigades from noon 30th June 1918.
   Brigade Dumps will be situated in the same positions as the reserve ammunition for the Reserve Battalions of the French Regiment in the Line, e.g.,

   Right Brigade.   M.5.a.3.5.
   Centre Brigade.   M.5.a.5.9.
   Left Brigade.   G.35.d.9.2.

   The ammunition to form these dumps will be delivered by the S.A.A.Section on the evening of the 29th June 1918, when Brigades will send forward a guard to take them over.

   By arrangement with the 7th French Division S.A.A. is being sent up to the Line on the 28th June and 29th June and will be dumped as follows :-

   For Right Front Line Battalion at   - M.18.c.8.0.   50 boxes.
   For Centre Front Line Battalion at - M.12.d.3.3.   50 boxes.
   For Left Front Line Battalion at   - N.7.c.5.6.   50 boxes.

   For Right Support Battalion at   - M.18.a.7.2.   50 boxes.
   For Centre Support Battalion at   - M.6.c.3.6.   50 boxes.
   For Left Support Battalion   at   - M.6.d.6.6.   50 boxes.

   Remainder of Battalion allotments and Light T.Mortar ammunition required, will be taken up under Brigade arrangements when carrying out the relief

/Arrangements

(2).

(b) S.A.A. and Grenades etc (continued)

Arrangements have been made with the 7th French Division for a sufficient number of French Pistols and S.O.S.signals to be left in the Line until the British S.O.S.signal is taken into use.
Brigades will arrange to take these over.
On the 2nd July 1918 they will be collected and returned to Divisional Headquarters for transmission to the French.

3. SUPPLIES.

Railhead - STEENVOORDE. from 29th instant.

The Divisional Train will draw from Railhead by horse transport from 30th instant and will deliver to units transport lines.
Battalion transport normally proceeds as far East as the following points :-
    Right Brigade.   M.11.d.8.6.
    Centre Brigade.   M.12.b.0.3.
    Left Brigade.   M.6.d.9.7.

Reserve rations are dumped in the area as follows :-

Right Brigade.	SCHERPENBERG TUNNELS.	Front Line Bn.	500 rations.
		Support Bn.	500 rations.
	G.27.d.4.3.	Reserve Bn.	500 rations.
Centre Brigade.	M.18.b.5.1.	Front Line	500 rations.
	M.12.c.9.4.	Support Bn.	500 rations.
Left Brigade.	N.7.c.2.3.	Front Line Bn.	500 rations.
	M.6.d.4.6.	Support Bn.	500 rations.

These rations will be taken over by Brigades on relief, and they will be responsible for their safe custody.

4. WATER.

The water supply in the Forward Area is poor, and is reported as being badly contaminated, the greatest care must therefore be taken as regards chlorination.
    There are water cart filling points
        REMY SIDING.
        S.W.of HOOGRAAF CABT.
        ABEELE STATION.
Barrel reservoirs have been made by the French :-
    Right Brigade.   M.11.b.6.2.
    Centre Brigade.   M.5.a.6.6.
    Left Brigade.   M.6.a.0.9.

Petrol tins will be issued on the following scale :-
    Brigade Headquarters   20
    Battalions.   220
    T.M.Bs.   20
    M.Gun Companies.   40*
    Field Co.R.E.   40*
    Pioneer Company.   40*
    Forward Fld Amblnce.   50

* If in positions where water carts cannot be used.

Instructions as to drawing will be issued later.

(3).

5. R.E. MATERIAL.

    Divisional Dump   STEENAKER. L.32.d.4.0.

Forward Stores will be arranged through Field Company Commanders in Brigade Sectors.

6. MEDICAL ARRANGEMENTS.

(A). Headquarters Forward Field Ambulance   WIPPENHOEK.L.28.d.5.6.
    (139th Field Ambulance)   Sheet 27.

i. Headquarters Forward Bearers and Collecting   G.21.c.5.9.
    Post, also Car Post.   Sheet 28.
    RENINGHELST-POP Road

ii. Collecting Post, also Car Post.   G.34.d.5.5. Sheet 28.
    (cellars of old 41st D.H.Q)

iii. Collecting Post, also Car Post.   ZEVECOTEN G.35.d.5.6.
    To be moved later when post is finally constructed to ZEVECOTEN SIDING YARD. at G.36.c.2.2. Sheet 28.

iv. Collecting Post.   M.5.b.6.1. Sheet 28.
    Relay Post.   M.11.central. Sheet 28.

v. Collecting Post.   M.18.a.1.8. Sheet 28.

(B). Main Dressing Station, Gas Centre
    & Sorting Station for Sick   REMY SIDING.
    140 h Field Ambulance.   Old site No.2 Canadian C.C.S.
    L.23.a.1.1.

(C). D.R.S. for sick and
    lightly wounded.   RWELD. L.27.b.3.2.
    (138th Fld Ambulance)
    (not open at present).

i. At present no Advanced Dressing Stations — cases will be sent from R.A.Ps. direct to Bearer Collecting Post and from thence direct in wheeled stretchers and Divisional cars to M.D.S. at REMY SIDING.

ii. All sick will be sent to M.D.S. REMY SIDING until the D.R.S. at RWELD can be organised and opened.

    Cars kept at No.1, 2, and 3, Collecting Posts REMY SIDING, WIPPENHOEK, and RWELD.

(D). R.A.P. will be notified later.

/7 (Provost

(4).

7. PROVOST INSTRUCTIONS.

(a). Traffic Control.

The A.P.M. will establish Traffic Control Posts at the following points :-

L.33.c.2.3.
L.34.d.0.3.
L.35.d.1.2.
G.32.d.8.2.

(b). Straggler Posts will be posted as follows if necessary :-

G.27.1.8.6.
G.32.d.8.2.
M.2.a.5.2.

One N.C.O. and 3 men will be detailed from the Reserve Battalion Right Brigade to report to M.M.P. at each of the above points on receipt of orders from Divisional Headquarters.

(c). Motor Headlights must be extinguished east of GODEWAERSWELDE - POPERINGHE Railway.
Sidelights east of LOYE Cross Roads.

(d). Lorries may not proceed further East than BOESCHEPE - WIPPENHOEK Road in daylight.
Horse Transport may not proceed further East than the N.& S. Grid Line between squares G.31 and 32 in daylight.

(e). Steel helmets and Box Respirators in the alert position, will be worn by all ranks East of the N.& S. Grid Line between squares G.31 and 32.

ACKNOWLEDGE.

June 28th 1918.

Lieut Colonel,
A.A. & Q.M.G.
41st Division.

Distribution as Operation Order 257
copy to MT Co.

TABLE "A".

(Reference Sheet 27, 1/40,000).

ACCOMMODATION.

Unit.	Personnel.	Transport. "A" Echelon.	"B" Echelon.
122nd I.Brigade.	Line (Left).	LAPPE	BEAUVORDE WOOD.
123rd I.Brigade.	Line (Centre.)	LOYE.	
124th I.Brigade.	Line (Right).	K.36.central.	L.26.a.1.4.
Machine G.Bn.	Line.	L.33.central.	K.31.b.1.8. / K.25.c.8.6.
- do - (Res Coy.)	L.23.c.1.2.		
Royal Engineers.	Line.		STEEN AKKER
- do - 1 Company	ABEELE AERODROME.		
19th Middlesex.	L.28.d.1.9.		STEEN AKKER
138th Field Amblnce.			RWELD
139th Field Amblnce.		WIPPENHOEK	RWELD
140th Field Amblnce.			REMY SIDING.
Divisional Train			
No.1 Company.			WATON FRANCE
No.2 Company. No.3 Company. No.4 Company.			ST ELOY.
Motile Vet Section			ST ELOY.

AMMUNITION TO BE HELD BY 41st DIVISION.   Schedule "F"

Where Held.	S.A.A.	T.M.A.	No.23 G'des.	No.24 G'des.	No.36 G'des.	V.L.1" White.	S.O.S.	STOKES T.M.	VARIOUS.
Each Battalion in Line.	100,000. (50 Boxes in Coy & Platoon Res. 50 Boxes Battn Reserve) Includes L.G. Reserve.		1000	750	500	1000	48		
Each Battalion in Support.	50,000. (25 Boxes in Coy & Platoon Res. 25 Boxes in Battn Reserve) Includes L.G. Reserve.		500	500		500	12		
Left & Centre Battalions in Reserve.	50,000 (25 Boxes in Coy & Platoon Res. 25 Boxes Battn Reserve) Includes L.G.								
Each Machine Gun Position.	10,000								
Each M.G. Dump.	200,000		1000	750	500	1000	24		
Divisional Dump	500,000		2000	1500	1000	2000	48	3,800 *	500 Smoke Rifle 500 Smoke Hand 20,000 S.A.A.A.P. 20,000 S.A.A. (Tracer) 1,750 Green Ctges 5,800 Ring Chgs.

* Original Establishment only to be drawn from IV.M.R. to complete reserve of 100 per T.M. in position.
200 Ring Charges " " " "
200 Green Ctges " " " "

1st. AMENDMENT TO 41st. DIVISION ADMINISTRATIVE
INSTRUCTION No.35 dated June 28th 1918.

Para 6. Medical Arrangements.

(A.iii). The map reference of Collecting Post at ZEVECOTEN should read C.35.c.5.6.

(B & C). Map references to M.D.S. and D.R.S. are sheet 27.

(A 1). The Collecting Post at G.21.c.5.9. is also a Post for Walking Wounded.

29/6/18.

Lieut.Colonel,
A.A.& Q.M.G.,
41st.Division.

Copies to all recipients of A.I.35.

APPENDIX E.

STATEMENT OF COURTS MARTIAL FOR JUNE, 1918.

41st DIVISION.

UNIT.	No. of Cases.	Charge.	Sentence.
12th E. Surrey Rgt.	1	Desertion.	3 years P.S.
15th Hampshire Rgt.	1	Absent without leave.	2 years I.H.L.
18th K.R.R.C.	1	do.	42 days F.P.1.
23rd Middlesex R.	4	3- Desertion.	1 - Death, Commuted to 15 years P.S. 1 - 3 years P.S. 1 - Not guilty.
		1- Absent without leave.	42 days F.P.1.
11th Queen's.	2	1- Conduct to prejudice of good order & Military discipline.	Not guilty.
		1- Absent without leave.	6 months I.H.L.
10th R.W. Kent R.	1	Conduct / Prejudice to good order & Military discipline.	28 days F.P.2.
20th Durham L.I.	1	Striking superior Officer.	90 days F.P.1.
41st Trench Mortar Bty. R.F.A.	1	Absent without leave.	1 year I.H.L.
187 Bde. R.F.A.	1	do.	90 days F.P.1.
41st Bn. M.G.C.	1	Playing cards with O.Rs.	Severe reprimand.
19th Middlesex R.	1	Insubordinate language to superior officer.	28 days F.P.1.

APPENDIX F

41st. DIVISION.

CASUALTIES AND SICK. JUNE 1918.

Unit.	Officers.			Other Ranks.			Sick Wastage.
	Killed.	Wounded.	Missing.	Killed.	Wounded.	Missing.	
12/E.Surrey.R.	-	-	-	3	14	-	72
1f/Hants.R.	-	-	-	1	5	-	73
18th.K.R.R.C.	-	-	-	-	-	-	55
11/Queens.	-	-	-	-	4	-	191
10th.R.W.Kents.	-	-	-	-	3	-	91
23/Middlesex.	-	-	-	-	4	2	102
10/Queens.	-	-	-	-	-	-	69
26.R.Fusiliers.	-	-	-	-	-	-	74
20/D.L.I.	-	-	-	-	-	-	138
41st.Bn.M.G.C.	-	1	-	-	22	-	67
19th.Middlesex.	-	1	-	5	1	-	119
187th.Bde.RFA.	-	-	-	-	6	-	77
190th.Bde.RFA.	-	3	-	2	22	-	39
D.A.C.	-	-	-	-	1	-	23
228th.Fld.Coy.	-	-	-	-	2	-	3
233rd. " "	-	-	-	-	-	-	8
237th. " "	-	-	-	-	1	-	25
139th.Fld.Amb.	-	-	-	-	-	-	3
139th.Fld.Amb.	-	-	-	-	-	-	4
140th. " "	-	-	-	-	-	-	6
238th.Emp.Coy.	-	-	-	-	-	-	6
41st.Signals.	-	-	-	-	-	-	9
Divl.Train.	-	-	-	-	-	-	45
Total.	-	5	-	11	83	2	1293

Army Form C. 2118.

WAR DIARY
or
INTELLIGENCE SUMMARY.
'A' and 'Q' 41st.Division.
July 1918.

(Erase heading not required.)

Instructions regarding War Diaries and Intelligence Summaries are contained in F. S. Regs., Part II. and the Staff Manual respectively. Title pages will be prepared in manuscript.

Place	Date	Hour	Summary of Events and Information	Remarks and references to Appendices
La Linge.	July 3rd.		Divisional Headquarters moved to a new camp behind ABEELE (K.24.c.2.3/Sheet 27).	
K.24.c.2.3. Sheet 27.	July 23rd.		Administrative Instructions issued in connection with Battalions of 27th American Division. undergoing "Period B" attachment to Brigades in Line.	"A"
			A statement shewing casualties is attached.	"B"
			A statement shewing Courts Martial is attached.	"C"
	26/8/18.			

Lieut.Colonel,
A.A.&.Q.M.G.,
41st.Division.

APPENDIX "A"

SECRET.

41st DIVISION ADMINISTRATIVE INSTRUCTION No. 38
issued in connection with 41st Division G/371/29/5
dated 23/7/18 and G.421/29/5 dated 24/7/18.

1. ACCOMMODATION.
Tents and Shelters have been asked for to accommodate battalions coming out of Line on relief by American battalions and these will be issued if required for the use of Companies withdrawn under 41st Division G.421/29/5 dated today., para.2.

2. SUPPLIES.
(a). The American battalions will bring rations up to and including consumption 27th.

(b). Supply wagons will be attached to Divisional Train and rations for consumption 28th and after will be drawn from Railhead under arrangements to be made by Divisional Train.

(c). American battalion attached to 123rd Infantry Brigade will use 123rd Brigade Refilling Point.
American Battalions attached to 122nd and 124th Infantry Brigade will use 124th Brigade Refilling Point.
Other units to the same Refilling Point as the unit to whom they are attached.

(d). American Rations will be the same as British Rations except one oz. coffee per head takes the place of the tea ration.

Approximate Ration Strength.	Offrs.	O.R.
1st Battalion 108th Inf.Regt.	20	850
3rd Battalion do	18	800
Transport same as British Bns.		

(e). 1st days rations and water for American Troops in the Line will be prepared and sent up with the units to whom they are attached and will not be kept separate.

Other days. Rations and water for the complete American Platoons, Companies, or Battalion will be sent up separately by American Transport and carrying parties but will accompany the rations of the unit to which they are attached.

3. TRANSPORT.
American Transport should be located as near as possible to the unit to which they are attached and a close liaison should be kept between their respective Transport Officers and QuarterMasters.
American Quartermaster's Stores and Kitchens should be located with their attached units' Quartermaster's stores.

Acknowledge..

Major,
D.A.A.G.
41st Division.
(British).

July 24th 1918.

Copy to 122/123/124/ Inf.Brigades.
 - do - Transport Officers.
19th Middlesex, 41st M.Gun Bn.
C.R.A., C.R.E., A.D.M.S.,
D.A.D.V.S., Signal Co., Divl Train.
S.S.O., A.P.M., 27th American Division.
"G".

SECRET.

41st DIVISION ADMINISTRATIVE INSTRUCTION No. 38
issued in connection with 41st Division G/371/29/5
dated 23/7/18 and G.421/29/5 dated 24/7/18.

1. ACCOMMODATION.
Tents and Shelters have been asked for to accommodate battalions coming out of Line on relief by American Battalions and these will be issued if required for the use of Companies withdrawn under 41st Division G.421/29/5 dated today., para.2.

2. SUPPLIES.
(a). The American Battalions will bring rations up to and including consumption 27th.

(b). Supply wagons will be attached to Divisional Train and rations for consumption 28th and after will be drawn from Railhead under arrangements to be made by Divisional Train.

(c). American Battalion attached to 123rd Infantry Brigade will use 123rd Brigade Refilling Point.
American Battalions attached to 122nd and 124th Infantry Brigade will use 124th Brigade Refilling Point.
Other units to the same Refilling Point as the unit to whom they are attached.

(d). American Rations will be the same as British Rations except one oz. coffee per head takes the place of the tea ration.

Approximate Ration Strength.	Offrs.	O.R.
1st Battalion 108th Inf.Regt.	20	850
3rd Battalion – do –	18	800
Transport same as British Bns.		

(e). 1st days rations and water for American Troops in the Line will be prepared and sent up with the units to whom they are attached and will not be kept separate.

Other days. Rations and water for the complete American Platoons, Companies, or Battalion will be sent up separately by American Transport and carrying parties but will accompany the rations of the unit to which they are attached.

3. TRANSPORT.
American Transport should be located as near as possible to the unit to which they are attached and a close liaison should be kept between their respective Transport Officers and Quartermasters.
American Quartermaster's Stores and Kitchens should be located with their attached units' Quartermaster's stores.

Acknowledge..

Major,
D.A.A.G.
41st Division.
(British).

July 24th 1918.

Copy to 122/123/124/ Inf.Brigades.
– do – Transport Officers.
19th Middlesex, 41st M.Gun Bn.
C.R.A., C.R.E., A.D.M.S.,
D.A.D.V.S., Signal Co., Divl Train.
S.S.O., A.P.M., 27th American Division.
"G".

S E C R E T.

ADDITION TO
41st DIVISION ADMINISTRATIVE INSTRUCTION No 28 ISSUED
IN CONNECTION WITH 41st DIVISION G371/29/5 DATED 22/7/18
AND G451/29/5 DATED 24/7/18.

1. **SOLIDIFIED ALCOHOL.** Solidifed Alcohol for American Troops will be provided by the Units to whom they are attached.

2. **PETROL TINS.** For American Units will be avilable to draw from Divisional R.A.A. Dump after 3 p.m. 25th inst. Scale as laid down for this Division. Tins will require cleansing.

3. **RATIONS.** American personnel proceeding to the Line on night of 25th instant, will carry rations for consumption 26th on the man. Rations for consumption 27th will be sent up on night of 26th.

ACKNOWLEDGE.

(sgd) E.G. Whatley
Major,
D.A.A.G.
41st Division.
(British).

25th July 1918.

S E C R E T.

ADDENDUM NO
41st DIVISION ADMINISTRATIVE INSTRUCTION NO 56 ISSUED
IN CONNECTION WITH 41st DIVISION G371/20/5 DATED
23/7/1918 and G421/20/5 DATED 24/7/18.

* * * * * * * * * * * * * * * * * * * *

1. **SOLIDIFIED ALCOHOL.** Solidified Alcohol for the American Troops will be provided by the Units to whom they are attached.

2. **PETROL TINS.** For American Units will be available to draw from Divisional S.A.A. Dump after 5 p.m. 25th instant. Scale as laid down for this Division. Tins will require cleansing.

3. **RATIONS.** American personnel proceeding to the line on night of 26th instant will carry rations for consumption 26th on the man. Rations for consumption 27th will be sent up on night of 26th.

ACKNOWLEDGE.

(sgd) E.G. Whateley.

Major,
D.A.A.G.
41st Division.
(British).

25th July, 1918.

Appendix "B"

41st. DIVISION.
CASUALTY AND SICK. JULY 1918.

Unit.	Officers. Killed.	Officers. Wounded.	Officers. Missing.	Other Ranks. Killed.	Other Ranks. Wounded.	Other Ranks. Missing.	Sick Wastage.
12/E.Surrey R.		2		9	35		28
1f/Hants.	1	1		13	58	2	28
18th.K.R.R.C.				4	40		26
11th.Queens.	1	4		11	72	5	43
10/R.W.Kents.		1		7	42		21
23/Middlesex.		2		2	45	10	21
10/Queens.	1	3		8	33		23
26/R.Fusrs.		2	1	7	35		27
20/H.L.I.		2		3	40	2	61
41st.M.G.C.		1		6	22	1	27
19th.Middlesex.		2		2	33		20
187th.Bde.R.F.A.				1	8		16
190th.Bde.R.F.A.				1	2		17
D.A.C.				1			17.
22 8th.Fld.Coy.				1	4		1
233rd.Field Coy.				1	4		6
237th Field Co.				1	2		5
158th Fld Ambulance.							5
159th Fld Ambulance.					3		6
140th Fld Ambulance.					5		5
238th Employment Co.					1		6
Signal Co.							4
Divisional Train.							1
	3	20	1	77	482	20	410

APPENDIX C

STATEMENT OF COURTS MARTIAL FOR JULY 1918.

41st DIVISION.

UNIT	No. of cases	CHARGE	SENTENCE
12th E.Surrey Regt.	2.	1- Desertion.	Death - commuted to 20 years P.S.
		1- Absent without leave.	90 days F.P.1.
15th Hampshire Regt.	2.	1- Negligently discharging firearms.	42 days F.P.2.
		1- Absent without leave.	21 days F.P.2.
18th K.R.R.C.	1	Insult.Language to Sup.Officer.	56 days F.P.1.
23/Middx.	7.	1- Drunkenness.	Not guilty.
		1- Absent without leave.	56 days F.P.1.
		3- Disobeying Lawful Cmnd.	1.- 90 days F.P.1.
			1 - 3 years P.S.
			1 - 46 days F.P.1.
		1- Desertion.	2 years I.H.L.
		1- Allowing prisoners to escape.	Not guilty.
10/R.W.Kent R.	1.	Absent without leave.	28 days F.P.1.
26/R.Fusiliers.	3.	1- Drunkenness.	56 days F.P.1.
		1- Absent without leave.	90 days F.P.1.
		1- Desertion.	Death.
20/Durham L.I.	1.	Neglect to prej. of Good Order and Mil.Disc.	Not Guilty.
10/Queens.	2.	1- Disobeying lawful Cmnd.	12 Mnths. I.H.L.
		1- Conduct to prej. of Good Order and Mil.Dis.	28 Days F.P.1.
187th.Bde.R.F.A.	1	Desertion.	3 years P.S.
41st.Bn.M.G.Corps.	1	Conduct to prej. of Good Order and Mil.Disc.	14 days F.P.2.
Divl.Train.	1	Refusing to obey an order.	42 days F.P.1.
R.E.Signals.	1	Contravention of Censorship Regs.	42 days F.P.2.

Army Form C. 2118.

WAR DIARY
or
INTELLIGENCE SUMMARY.

"A" & "Q" 41st. Division.

August 1918.

(Erase heading not required.)

Instructions regarding War Diaries and Intelligence Summaries are contained in F. S. Regs., Part II. and the Staff Manual respectively. Title pages will be prepared in manuscript.

Place	Date	Hour	Summary of Events and Information	Remarks and references to Appendices
K.24.c.2.3.	Aug.27.		Administrative Instructions issued in connection with move of the Division by rail and bus to training area THIEQUES.	'A'
	Aug.30th.		Divisional Headquarters closed at K.24.c.2.3. and re-opened at WIZERNES same day.	
			A statement shewing casualties and sick evacuations for the month of August.	'B'
			A statement shewing Courts Martial for the month of August.	'C'
	20/9/18.		[signature]
Lieut.Colonel,
A.A.& Q.M.G.,
41st.Division.	

41st DIVISION.

CASUALTIES AND SICK EVACUATIONS — AUGUST 1918.

Unit.	OFFICERS Killed.	Wounded.	Missing.	O.Ranks Killed.	Wounded.	Missing.	Sick Wastage.
12th.E.Surrey R.	1	3	-	17	59	13	37
15th.Hants.R.	2	5	-	25	127	27	32
18th.K.R.R.C.	6	3	-	16	79	21	46
11th.Queens.	-	-	-	9	35	-	53
10th.R.W.Kent R.	-	6	-	3	31	3	29
23rd.Middlesex.	1	-	-	15	55	-	31
10th.Queens.	1	1	-	6	29	-	40
26th.R.Fusiliers.	-	1	-	2	31	1	49
20th.D.L.I.	-	1	-	2	24	1	41
19th.Middlesex.	-	1	-	2	13	1	31
41st.Bn.M.G.Corps.	-	-	-	5	25	1	53
187th.Bde.R.F.A.	-	-	-	1	5	-	21
190th.Bde.R.F.A.	-	3	-	1	13	-	20
41st.D.A.C.&T.M.B.	1	-	-	-	-	-	9
228th.Fld.Coy.R.E.	-	1	-	1	18	-	4
233rd.Fld.Coy.R.E.	-	-	-	2	5	-	8
237th.Field Coy.R.E.	-	1	-	1	-	-	6
138th.Fld.Amb.	-	-	-	-	2	-	3
139th.Fld.Amb.	-	-	-	-	-	-	11
140th.Fld.Amb.	-	-	-	-	4	-	6
41st.Divl.Sig.Coy.	-	1	-	-	1	-	6
Divl.Train.	-	-	-	1	-	-	3
52nd.M.V.S.	-	-	-	-	-	-	1
238th.Emp.Coy.	-	-	-	-	-	-	5
	10	28	2	103	544	48	524

41st. DIVISION.

COURTS MARTIAL FOR THE MONTH OF AUGUST 1918.

Unit.	No. of Cases.	Charge.	Sentence.
18th.K.R.R.C.	1	Stealing public goods.) Absent without leave.)	4 years P.S.
23rd.Middx.	4	1. Insub.Language.	18 mnths I.H.L.
		1. Neglect to pred. of good order and Mil.Dis.	28 days F.P.2.
		1. Disobeying orders.	Notguilty.
		1. Drunkenness.	Not Guilty.
10th.R.W.Kents.	2.	1. Absent without leave.	Reduced to rks.
		1. Making false statement.	70 days F.P.1.
20th.D.L.I.	4.	1. Leaving Post.	90 days F.P.1.
		2. Breaking in House.	1. 1 yr. I.H.L.
			1. 3 yrs. P.S.
		1. Conduct to pred. of good order and military discipline.	60 days F.P.1.
26th.R.Fusrs.	4.	3. - do -	1. 35 days F.P.2.
			1. 90 " F.P.1.
			1. 56 " " " "
		1. Absent without leave.	18 mnths I.H.L.
10th.Queens.	1.	Disobeying lawful commnd.	56 days F.P.1.
41st.Bn.M.G.C.	1.	Stealing officers kit.	6 mnths I.H.L.

AMENDMENT TO 41st.DIVISIONAL ADMINISTRATIVE
INSTRUCTION No.40 DATED 27th.AUGUST 1918.
TABLE 'D'.

Field Ambulance (122 Bde)	—	to BOISDINGHEM.
Field Ambulance (124 Bde)	—	not proceeding.
Field Ambulance (123 Bde)	—	to LONGUENESSE instead of St.MARTIN AU LAERT.
Field Coy. (122 Bde)	—	to HALLINES.
Coy.Divl.Train.(123 Bde).	—	to St.MARTIN AU LAERT.
D.A.C.	—	to TILQUES.
M.M.S.	—	to VIZERNES.

ACKNOWLEDGE.

Major,
D.A.A.G., 41st.Division.

28/8/18.

Issued to all recipients of 41st.Divl. : No.40 dated 27/8/18.
Instr.

War Diary 'A'

SECRET.
****

41st Division Administrative Instruction No.40
issued in connection with 41st Division Order No.266
dated August 27th 1918.

1. (a). The personnel of the Division (less Artillery) will be conveyed to the WILQUES Area by rail and bus in accordance with attached Table "A".

    (b). No kit other than trench bundles can be taken on the trains or busses, and arrangements must be made to send all kit other than this to transport lines on the night before relief.

    (c). Personnel will be at the entraining or embussing point at least three quarters of an hour before scheduled hour of departure, and each unit on arrival will report its presence to the Officer in charge of entrainment or embussment.

    (d). Arrangements will be made for bivouac areas close to the entraining or embussing point where units arriving early can wait.

    (e). Officer in charge of entrainment :- a/D.A.Q.M.G.
    Officer in charge of Detrainment :- D.A.A.G.

2. (a). The Divisional Train, S.A.A.Section D.A.C., Mobile Veterinary Section, and First Line Transport of units will move to the WILQUES Area by march route in accordance with attached March Table "B", staging for night at RENESCURE. Billets from Area Commandant RENESCURE, to whom officer should report in advance of column.

    (b). The Officer Commanding the Train Company will be in Command of the Column in each case.

    (c). The A.P.M. will detail a proportion of M.M.P. to accompany each column.

    (d). Brigades and units can arrange with Officer Commanding Train Company concerned for cookers and water carts to meet troops at detraining stations if they desire to do so and time permits.

3. (a). Supply Railhead changes to LUMBRES on 31st August.

    (b). On 29th August supplies for troops proceeding on night 28th/29th will be drawn by M.T. and delivered in WILQUES area.
    On 30th August supplies for troops in WILQUES Area and for those proceeding there on night 29th/30th will be drawn by M.T. and delivered in WILQUES Area.
    On 31st August and 1st September supplies for troops proceeding on night 31st/1st will be drawn by M.T. and delivered in WILQUES area.
    On 2nd September the whole Divisional Train will draw by H.T. from LUMBRES.

3. (c). On 27th August train will deliver rations for consumption 28th/and 29th to troops proceeding to new area on night 28th/29th.

On 28th August train will deliver rations for consumption 29th and 30th to troops proceeding to new area on night 29th/30th.

On 30th August train will deliver rations for consumption 31st and 1st to troops proceeding to new area on night 31st/1st.

As the transport leaves the day before its unit, arrangements must be made to issue the two days rations to the men on the night before the transport leaves.

4. Baggage wagons will report to units on the morning of the day before they march.

Additional transport has been asked for in accordance with attached Table "C".

5. On arrival in WILQUES Area the Division will be accommodated as shown in attached Table "D".

6. Relief of Traffic Control personnel will take place on 29th instant under arrangements to be made by A.P.M's.

7. The Salvage Section of the Employment Company, S.A.A. Section 41st D.A.C., and Ammunition Dump, Divisional Baths, and Divisional Canteen will be relieved at 12 noon on the 29th instant.

8. All ammunition, petrol tins (in excess of Mobile Establishment), balance of week's allotment of solidified alcohol, gum boots, gas clothing, pack saddles, water tins, and all trench stores will be handed over to the 34th Division on relief and a copy of receipts sent to Divisional Headquarters.

9. All camps and billets will be handed over in a thoroughly clean and sanitary condition.

10. Divisional Baths and Canteen close in the present area on the evening of the 28th instant.

August 27th 1918.

Lieut Colonel,
A.A. & Q.M.G.
41st Division.

Copy to :- 122nd Brigade.
123rd Brigade.
124th Brigade.
C.R.A. (for information).
C.R.E.
19th Middlesex.
41st M.Gun Bn.
Signal Co.
Camp Commandant.
Divl Baths Offr.
O.C.Canteen.
Posts.
D.A.D.O.S.
34th Division.
Entraining Offrs 2 Copies.

Divisional Train.
S.S.O.
41st M.T.Company.
A.D.M.S.
A.P.M.
D.A.D.V.S.
2nd Mob Vet Section.
Employment Co.
"G".
41st Reception Camp.
Salvage Officer.
War Diary.
XIXth Corps Q.
Area Commdt RENESCURE.

SCHEDULE A. (1). (BROAD GUAGE).

SERIAL NO.	DATE.	UNITS.	ENTRAINMENT.	DETRAINMENT.	DEPART.	ARRIVE.	REMARKS.
1.	28/29.	12/E.Surrey Rgt. 1/Hants Rgt. 18/K.R.R.Corps.	ABEELE.	LUMBRES.	8 a.m. 29th.	8 a.m.	Total entraining strength = 1900
2.	29/30.	23/Middlesex Rgt. 237th.Coy.R.E. 139th.Field Amb. H.Qrs. & 2 Coys. Pioneers. Remainder Divl H.Qrs Divl Sig.Coy. Headquarters, & 1 Coy. M.G.battn.	ABEELE.	St.OMER.	4 a.m. 30th.	9 a.m.	Total entraining strength = 1950.
3.	31/1st.	124th.Bde.H.Qrs. 10/Queens. 228th.Field Coy.R.E. 140th.Field Amb. 2 Coy's M.G.battn.	ABEELE.	LUMBRES.	4 a.m. 1st.	9 a.m.	Total entraining strength = 1500.

SCHEDULE "A2" LIGHT RAILWAYS.

Serial No.	Date.	Unit.	Entrain at. LOYE.	Change at. WINNEZEELE.	Detrain at. POPERINH.	Time entrain at.	Time change.	Time arrive
1	29/30	123 Brigade Hd-Qrs. 220 all ranks 11/Queens.				6.12 a.m.	11.27 am.	2.27. pm.
2	29/30	360 all ranks 11/Queens.	do.	do.	do.	6.15 a.m.	12.07 pm.	3.7. pm.
3	29/30	Remainder 11/Queens. 330 all ranks 10/Kents.	do.	do.	do.	6.30 a.m.	12.47 pm.	3.47 pm.
4.	29/30	Remainder 10/Kents. 123 L.T.M.Bty.	do.	do.	do.	6.45 a.m.	1.27 pm.	4.27 pm.
1	31/1st.	350 all ranks 26/R.Fusrs.	do.	do.	do.	6.12 a.m.	11.27 am.	2.27 pm.
2	31/1st.	Remainder 26/R.Fusiliers.	do.	do.	do.	6.15 a.m.	12.07 p.m.	3.7 pm.
3	31/1st.	390 all ranks 20/D.L.I.	do.	do.	do.	6.30 a.m.	12.37 pm.	3.37 pm.
4	31/1st.	Remainder 20/D.L.I. 124 L.T.M.Bty.	do.	do.	do.	6.45 a.m.	1.27 pm.	4.27 pm.

Serial Nos. 1 & 2, Aug. 29/30th and Aug 31/Sept 1st - Train consists of 12 trucks each accommodating 30 all ranks.

Serial Nos. 3 & 4, Aug. 29/30th and Aug. 31/Sept 1st - Train consists of 13 trucks each accommodating 30 all ranks.

SCHEDULE A.5.   BUSSES.
※※※※※※※※※※※※※※※※※※※※※※※※※※※※※

Serial No. of Column.	Date.	Units.	Embus at	Debus at.	Time top.	Time arrive.	Remarks.
1	28th/29th.	122nd Bde.H.Qrs. 23rd Fld.Coy.R.E. 1 Coy.M.G.Batth. 1 Coy. Pioneers. Portion Divl.H.Q. Divl.Observers. 138th Fld.Amb.co.	Head of Column L.34.d.1.7. facing South.	ESQUERDES.	10.p.m.	2.0.p.m.	Column consists of 35 lorries. 138th Field Ambulance will be picked up on Main STEENVOORDE-CASSEL Road about 1½ kilometres WEST of CASSEL. The last 5 lorries of column will be left vacant for this purpose.

TABLE "B". For Transport. (Ref Sheet 27.)

Serial No.	Date	Units.	Line of Start.	Starting Point.	From	To.	Route.	Remarks.
1	28th	No.2 Co.Div Train in order of march. 1st L.4pt 122 I.B. 233 Fld Co 138 Fld Amb. 2 Cos Pioneers 1 Co.M.G.Bn. Signal Co. Divl H.Qtrs.	2.p.m.	Road Junct P.3.k.6.3.	Present Area	RENESCURE	QUAESTRAETE - OXELAERE - HAVINGHOVE - LE NIEPPE.	Fighting limbers M.G.Coy and Lewis Gun limbers of Battns will remain to bring guns from Lino.
1	29th	Serial No.1.	8.a.m.	—	RENESCURE	TILQUES Area.	ARQUES - St OMER.	
2.	29th	H.Q.& No.3 Co.Train 1st L.4pt 123 I.B. 237 Fld Co. 1st L.4pt.138 Fld Amb. Pioneers less 2 Cos. H.Q.& 1 Co. M.Gun Bn. S.A.A.Sec D.A.C. 2 M.Vet Sec.	2.30.p.m.	Cross Rds. P.2.d.7.8.	Present Area	RENESCURE	QUAESTRAETE OXELAERE HAVINGHOVE LE NIEPPE	Fighting Limbers M.G.Co. and Lewis Gun Limbers of Battns will remain to bring guns from Lino.
2.	30th	Serial No.2.	8.a.m.		RENESCURE	TILQUES AREA	ARQUES - St OMER	

Sheet 2. (March Table).

Serial	Units in order of march.	Time of Start.	Starting Point.	From.	To	Route.	Remarks.
Serial No.2.	No.4 Coy. Train Batte 31stle t L. & t 124 I.B. " " 228 Fld Co. " " 140th Fld Amb. " " Coys M.G.Bn.	2.p.m.	Road Junct P.3.b.6.3.	Present Area	RENESCURE	QUA.S.TRAETE OXELAERE HAVINGHOVE LE NIEPPE	Fighting Limbers M.G.Bn., Lewis gun Limbers of Battle 124 Bde remain to bring guns from Line.
Serial No.3.		8.a.m.	LACROSSE A.9.c.4.0.	RENESCURE	TILQUES AREA	ARQUES ST.OMER	

NOTE. 1. Normal distances between units and vehicles as laid down in Second Army Area will be maintained throughout.

2. Fighting Limbers Machine Gun Companies and Lewis Gun Limbers of Battalions which remain behind to take guns from Line, will march the day after for other transport of group by same route and stages.

TABLE "C".

Date.	No. of Lorries.	Reporting at.	Time.	Unit for whom required.
28th	1	Embussing Point K.34.c.9.3.	8.a.m.	Advanced parties 122nd Brigade Group.
Total	4	Embussing Point K.34.c.9.3.	9.a.m.	Packs of 12th E.Surrey and 1/th Hants.
6.	1	138th Fld Amb Ince J.27.b.3.2.	12 noon	138th Field Ambulance.
29th	1	DREEF Cross Roads L.34.d.1.3.	1.a.m	122nd Inf Bde F.Qtrs.
Total	1	Embussing Point K.34.c.9.3.	3.a.m.	Advanced Party 123rd Bde Group.
21	6.	Embussing Point K.34.c.9.3.	8.a.m.	Packs of 123rd Inf Brigade.
	9.	Divisional H.Qtrs. K.24.c.2.3.	8.a.m.	Moving D.H.Qtrs.
	2.	Divl H.Qtrs. K.24.c.2.3.	9.a.m.	M.Gun Bn. and Packs of M.G.Bn.
	1.	Divl H.Qtrs. K.24.c.2.3.	9.a.m.	Divl Observation Section.
	1.	139th Fld Amb Ince L.28.d.7.6.	12 noon	139th Fld Ambulance.
30th	1.	DREEF Cross Roads L.34.d.1.3.	2.a.m.	123rd Inf Bde H.Qtrs.
Total	1.	DREEF Cross Rds. L.34.d.1.3.	2.a.m.	123rd L.T.M.Btty.
3.	1.	19th Middlesex H.Q. L.28.d.0.7.	12 Midnight	19th Middlesex Pioneers.
31st	1.	Embussing Point K.34.c.9.3.	3.a.m.	Advanced Parties 124th Brigade Group.
Total	6.	Embussing Point K.34.c.9.3.	9.a.m.	Packs of 124th Inf Brigade.
8.	1.	140th Fld Amb Inco L.22.d.9.4.	12 noon	140th Fld Amb Ince.
1st	1.	DREEF Cross Rds. L.34.d.1.3.	2.a.m.	124th Inf Bde H.Qtrs.
Total 2	1.	DREEF Cross Rds. L.34.d.1.3.	2.a.m.	124th L.T.M.Btty.

Guides from units to meet lorries at rendezvous.

=*=*=*=*=*=*=*=*=*=*=*=*=*=*=*=*=*=

TABLE "D".

ACCOMMODATION.

Units.	Area	Approximate Accommodation. Offrs / O.Rks.
Divl H.Qtrs.	WIZERNES	
122nd Brigade.	**(A). ESQUERDES Sub Area.**	
H.Q.	HALLINES	30 / 700
1 Bn.	SEQUES (Baths).	50 / 1100
1 Bn.	FERSINGHEM and	8 / 550
1 Bn.	ESQUERDES	50 / 1400
Field Co.	SEQUES	
Field Amblnce.	HALLINES	
Co.Divl Train.	GONDARDENNE	
L.M.B.	SEQUES	
Spare.	ACQUIN (C.Area).	28 / 698
123rd Brigade.	**(B). ST MARTIN AU LAERT. Sub Area.**	
H.Qtrs & 1 Bn.	WATINGHEM	40 / 1100
1 Bn.	ST MARTIN AU LAERT.	45 / 1100
1 Bn.	WIZERNES (A) Area. (Baths).	40 / 1000
Fld Co.	LONGUENESSE	20 / 500
Fld Amblnce.	ST MARTIN AU LAERT	
Co.Divl Train.	TILQUES	35 / 1000
L.M.B.	LONGUENESSE	
124th Brigade.	**(C). BOISDINGHEM Sub Area.**	
H.Qtrs.	BOISDINGHEM	
1 Bn.	(MORINGHEM	15 / 330
	(P DIFQUES	15 / 550
	(G DIFQUES	7 / 210
1 Bn.	(ZUDAUSQUES	13 / 400
	(NOIR CARME ADSOI L.LIHEUSE.	15 / 370
	(BARLINGHEM	3 / 360
1 Bn.	QUELLES (A Area).	29 / 920
Fld Co.	ZUTOVE	12 / 150
Fld Amblnce.	BOISDINGHEM	28 / 500
Train Co.	QUERCAMP	20 / 600
L.M.B.	QUERCAMP	
M.Gun Bn. H.Qtrs.	SALPERWICK) (B.Area).	20 / 600
	SCADERBOURG)	15 / 500
Pioneers.	LEULINE	8 / 160
	AUDENTHUN	6 / 360
	ETERHEM	12 / 550
	LIULINGHEM	6 / 250
No.4 Co. Train.	WATAU FRANCE	

Adjustment of smaller units in Brigade Groups may be made in consultation with Area Commandants if desired, at ESQUERDES, ST MARTIN AU LAERT, and BOISDENGHEM respectively.

A Bath will be established in the BOISDENGHEM Area - the one at ACQUIN is dry.

www.ingramcontent.com/pod-product-compliance
Lightning Source LLC
Chambersburg PA
CBHW081550160426
43191CB00011B/1888